A review

Richard Fox in his new publication 'Making Relationships Work at Work – A toolkit for getting more done with less stress' is a useful and practical book for those who are looking to freshen up their work practices. There is also a bit of a clue in the title, it's about helping all of us to be less stressed and more in tune with our colleagues, and able to make our work place a creative and productive space.

There are lots of practical examples of how things can go wrong that will appeal to anyone who is used to reflective learning. Don't we all know how organisations and meetings can be the worst experiences of our lives. Richard is utterly practical, and the solutions are equally grounded in actual experience. As he says, this is probably the first book that moves through the foundations to more detailed engagement around building effective relationships. What is obvious is that this book is written by a practitioner for practitioners. You get the question and the answer. If anything, there is too much ground covered. But it is clear that Richard is a mentor and coach, and this shines through the pages of the book. Gently encouraging here, guiding there, it is entirely focused on getting the reader through to the next stage.

I was particularly drawn to the section on home working as we have all had to learn new and exciting things about the strengths as well as the weaknesses of home working. Here I think Richard is on the cusp of something new and exciting. As we have all endured the early days of a pandemic, we have all had to adjust to new ways of being in community and new ways of communicating. The principles that Richard suggests throughout this book should enable us to begin working in refreshed, but different ways. We need to go back and re-examine the assumptions we have made about our colleagues, our workplace and our way of working. What will be the new 'new'?

Who better to guide us through into new territory than someone who has spent a lifetime navigating new pastures and different contexts? As we move into an uncertain time of potentially significant change, we need the wise counsel and the steady hand of someone like Richard. Think of this book as a handy reference book that you can dip into when a new situation arises. Use it and reflect, then use it again. This book is a gift to come back to again and again.

Bob Fyffe
General Secretary, CTBI

Endorsements continued from the back cover

This book is very timely as making relationships work will be one of the key issues we will need to focus on while our working structures, securities and beliefs are being challenged.

The principles and tips in this practical book will enable young professionals to go through their working lives much more smoothly. As a seasoned professional I acquired many useful insights to apply in my work.

This is an excellent toolkit and a great read and not just for someone interested in 'making relationships work at work'.

Anke Neale, Head of Human Resources, MAKINO
Europe GmbH

I cannot recommend this book too highly for anyone in – or contemplating being in – a leadership role. There are lots of books in this crowded marketplace trying to give wise counsel. In my view this is by far the most practical and capable of speedy implementation. If you read this book and try out some of the practical tips which it contains, I am confident that you will soon see some real, tangible benefits.

Ken Woffenden has held many senior leadership roles
during his 40-year career in major legal practices

MAKING
RELATIONSHIPS
WORK AT WORK

**A toolkit for
getting more done
with less stress**

RICHARD FOX

First published in Great Britain by Practical Inspiration Publishing, 2020

© Richard Fox, 2020

© Chapter 5 and 15, Anneliese Guérin-LeTendre, 2020

The moral rights of the author have been asserted

ISBN   978-1-78860-173-3 (print)
          978-1-78860-172-6 (epub)
          978-1-78860-171-9 (mobi)

Practical Inspiration
PUBLISHING

Contents

About this book

This book is for you if you want to make your working week more enjoyable, productive and fulfilling, by learning what you can do to build great relationships, make the most of your skills, experience and personal qualities, and enhance your team's performance. You will also find this book useful if you are curious to find out more about your own preferred ways of being and working – and why you find working with some colleagues so effortless (almost not like working at all) while others drain your energy and leave you at a loss as to what to do next!

More specifically, this book is for you if you are:

> ➤ a member of a department or team who is committed to getting things done and creating harmonious and effective relationships at work, but you are not able to access a comprehensive training programme in interpersonal relationships

> ➤ an HR or Learning and Development professional, mentor or coach, who is looking for a resource handbook to give to workshop participants

> ➤ an experienced and capable professional stepping up to your first or a more senior management/ leadership position

This book will also be useful if you are:

> ➤ an existing director or manager keen to improve your interpersonal skills and enhance those of your team

> ➤ self-employed, working with some key associates. You want to know more about building good relationships and working collaboratively with business colleagues and clients

Many of the points in this book apply equally to external relationships and personal relationships.

Common-sense reasons for getting relationships right

People who get on well are much more likely to work well together and be willing to collaborate effectively. On the other hand, when staff are not engaged or feel unsupported at work, performance suffers, staff morale drops and staff turnover increases.

As you have probably read in the media, stress and mental ill health are now among the biggest causes of absence from work, so paying attention to building good relationships at work becomes a priority.

A book full of proven tips

You will notice in the following chapters that I use the words 'we' and 'us' throughout this book to reflect that most of my professional work has been delivered working collaboratively with others and to honour the fact that I have learned a lot from working well with my business partner, associates and clients.

I have pooled our joint experience of working in and with organisations, in over 20 countries, from start-ups to global organisations, in the public and private sectors and in virtually every industry sector. I've been fortunate to work with wonderful clients, across several continents – people like you! Based on the kinds of obstacles to good relationships that they've brought to training workshops and coaching sessions, and my own experiences of running departments and teams, this book offers practical strategies and tools to help you build and maintain great working relationships, manage challenging relationships – and stay confident and resilient in today's high-pressured and rapidly-changing work environments.

Why this? Why now?

We spend so much of our time at work – often more time with colleagues than with partners and families – so it's important to feel that the work environment is a positive, happy place to be. Through my professional work, I know the contaminating influence of poor working relationships, and the way in which they can affect the individual's general well-being, even impacting on mental health. I've also noticed that no matter how challenging the work environment may be, when people feel appreciated and valued, connected with their team and their organisation, work is more fulfilling and enjoyable, and they are more effective in their work.

Like my clients, you are probably eager to find practical solutions to interpersonal challenges which are making work a difficult place to be – and getting in the way of your team's success. You'll also notice how skills normally treated as stand-alone topics all connect with each other. However, I won't be offering any quick fixes or easy tricks – long term these don't fool anyone. Really effective team members speak and listen from the heart and building great relationships requires sustained effort.

Outline of the book

The 15 chapters of this book follow a logical progression, from 'Building the foundations' to 'Succeeding in special circumstances', so if your reading preference is for starting at the beginning and working through to the end, here's what this will feel like:

Part one		
1. It's all about relationships 2. Foundation stone – rapport and trust 3. Is it just me? Different personalities 4. Mind-sets and relationships 5. Communicating from the inside out 6. Listening heart and soul	**Building the foundations**	The must haves
Part two		
7. How are we going to work together? 8. No-con, no-sham influencing 9. Motivating myself and others 10. My best self – managing strengths 11. Feedback for learning 12. Delegating without resentment	**Handling the everyday stuff**	Want to have
Part three		
13. Working in dispersed or virtual teams 14. Managing difficult relationships 15. Valuing diverse cultures Stepping up toolkit	**Succeeding in special circumstances**	Will need to have

On the other hand, if you prefer to dip into a book and read specific chapters as you need them, that's fine too – you'll find what you need in just a few minutes (that's even faster than surfing the net). Just one word of caution though – remember that the foundational elements need to be in place for your working relationships to be successful – for example, giving feedback is less likely to go well if you don't have a trusting relationship. For this reason, I've placed certain 'must haves' right at the beginning of the book.

Each chapter includes one or more opportunities to 'Pause for reflection' where we invite you to relate what you have been reading to your own work experiences. Each chapter ends with brief sections called 'Applying this to your workplace' and 'Further references'.

Four reasons to have this toolkit for building great working relationships on your bookshelf:

➢ As far as I'm aware, *Making relationships work at work – a toolkit for getting more done with less stress* is the only book that comprehensively covers the main A–Z components of building and maintaining effective relationships at work

➢ This is a practical book, based on widely accepted theories and what works in real life, covering common issues frequently raised by coaching clients and workshop participants in recent years

➢ Most of the topics have been taught on several continents and have been well received so you can be confident of its universal application across national and professional cultures

➢ Connections have been made between topics in this book that are normally treated as stand-alone subjects, e.g. motivation and delegation. These linkages will make each topic more useful to you.

Acknowledgements

First, I would like to thank my friend and professional coach, Anneliese Guérin-LeTendre, who has provided invaluable practical support and encouragement throughout the writing of this book. I would also like to thank her for contributing Chapters 5 'Communicating from the inside out', and 15 'The riches of diversity'.

Second, I would like to thank my business partner, Ray Lamb, and our long-standing associate, Heather Brown, for their enormous support and encouragement, and all the clients and associates I have worked with over the years and who are the inspiration for this book.

Finally, I would also like to thank those clients and business leaders who offered to read and endorse the book, and my wife for her continued encouragement and support.

I trust that you will find this voyage of discovery interesting, enjoyable and useful. Please let me know how you get on.

Richard Fox
The Learning Corporation LLP
Surrey, UK
March 2020

Part one

Building the foundations: the must haves

1

It's all about relationships

What counts can't always be counted; what can be counted doesn't always count.

Albert Einstein, scientist

Introduction

One of our basic human needs is to have good relationships – not only in our personal lives but also at work. We spend most of our waking hours at work and our effectiveness and happiness depend heavily on the effectiveness of our work relationships. Whatever the advantages and joys of social media, it is through our personal connections with other people – at home and at work – that we satisfy our need for face-to-face relationships and a true feeling of belonging.

Relationship skills are often referred to as 'soft skills', a term which can cover quite a broad spectrum of activities, ranging from taking personal responsibility and using time effectively to influencing and handling conflict, but which all depend on, and are connected to, good communication. From engineering and manufacturing, to services and retail, within the private and the public sectors, all organisations rely for their success on good relationships, and no matter what your work focus, when it comes to making things happen, 'it's all about relationships' and good relationships are built through effective interpersonal skills. How we relate with each other determines whether teams come together or not; projects work out well, or don't; whether team members feel fulfilled and motivated, or don't!

The key points we cover in this chapter are:

➢ Relationship skills are as important as technical skills and usually more difficult to master

➢ As you progress through your working life you will need to spend more of your working day on relationships

➢ An understanding of Emotional Intelligence is essential to a productive and enjoyable working life

Using soft skills effectively

Typically, individuals who use soft skills effectively are genuinely interested in other people, are approachable and trustworthy. You'll have noticed that they share other personality traits, skills and abilities in common too – including the ability to:

➢ listen well

➢ communicate effectively

➢ be positive

➢ manage conflict

➢ accept responsibility

➢ show respect

➢ work well with colleagues

➤ manage emotions

➤ work well under pressure[1]

At the beginning of a career these 'soft skills' can appear to take a secondary position behind the so-called 'hard skills' relating to technical expertise, particularly if these technical skills have taken some years of education and training to acquire. Nevertheless, the quality of 'soft skills' between members of a team can either facilitate individuals' technical know-how – or undermine their best efforts. These skills are as complex and often prove to be every bit as difficult to master as the 'hard skills' such as engineering, IT systems or financial computations.

This book aims to give practical insights and solutions to managing the complexity of working relationships. We'll be looking at the kind of situations and challenges you encounter regularly and taking a closer look at how you can use your interpersonal skills to build and maintain positive relationships at work, fulfil your own potential, and make your contribution to building the team.

Your network of working relationships

Our relationships in the workplace can be considered from different perspectives:

---

[1] Report, *Soft skills in the UK economy*, Development Economics Ltd, 2015.

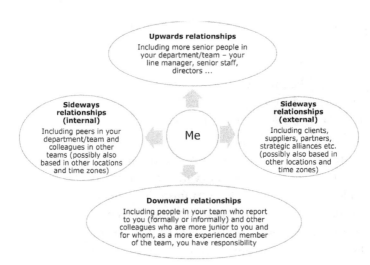

Your relationship networks

Depending on your experience and personality type you may prefer to build relationships with people in only two or three of the above dimensions. For example, you may prefer to keep your head down, get on with your own work and only talk to members of your team and your line manager on a 'need to know basis'. It is important, however, if you want to feel more secure in your job or progress your career, to build effective relationships with colleagues in each of the above four dimensions. Whilst reading this book we invite you to discover strategies to enable you to work more easily with colleagues in all four dimensions of your relationship network.

Besides having working relationships with individuals, you also have a personal relationship with the organisation itself. The quality of this relationship usually depends on whether your own values – integrity, honesty, openness, fairness and respect – are aligned with those of the organisation where you work and are assumed and visible in the way people behave throughout the organisation.

From task focus to relationship focus

As you gain experience in the organisation you notice that you need to spend an increasing amount of your time on relationships.

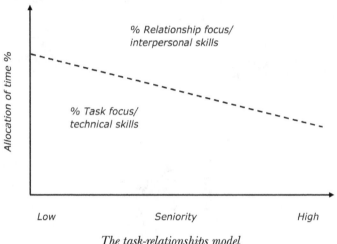

The task-relationships model

When you first started work you probably joined in a junior position. Depending on your industry sector you may have spent as much as 80% of your time on tasks associated with gaining the knowledge, skills and expertise in your field, with the remainder on relationships, mainly with other members of your team and with the client/manager to whom you were assigned.

As you progress in the organisation you are increasingly likely to lead and manage people; CEOs probably spend up to 80% of their time on building and maintaining relationships – internal and external – with a relatively small 20% on tasks. This shift from an operational to a strategic focus can sometimes be a challenge, especially if you have not mastered the art of delegation (Chapter 12). If you are on this journey where you're moving away from the familiar work role and routine and towards a slightly different work identity you may have moments of self-doubt and temporary loss of confidence. However, remember that your people skills and your ability to build solid lasting relationships at work are the constant that will stay with you and help you through changes in your job role.

The 'go-to' people

Experienced colleagues with good people skills
create 'hubs' of influence around them

Some colleagues, those with experience and know-how – whether in official roles of responsibility or not – are frequently, and rightly, sought out by colleagues. We like to think of these people as 'hubs' – the 'go-to' people who are approachable and inspire trust – in many ways these colleagues hold teams and organisations together. Although they are not necessarily leaders or managers, they are the kind of colleagues who always seem to be able to make time to listen, suggest, advise or support – perhaps you're one of them.

Whatever your role and contribution within the team or the organisation, from Day 1 'relationships' are as important to your job, your security in the organisation and your prospects for promotion as the 'tasks' you perform and the service you deliver. Equally important (more important for some people), the quality of your relationships at work creates that sense of belonging and connection so essential to having a sense of well-being and happiness at work. As we will see later in Chapter 9, the feeling of belonging, being accepted and valued for who you are, not just what you do, is often more motivating than money.

Using Emotional Intelligence

We are all familiar with IQ, the Intelligence Quotient, but as we go through life we recognise that:

> ➢ IQ is a narrow measure of intelligence

> ➢ People with a high IQ are not necessarily happier or more successful

> ➢ There are other forms of intelligence – Emotional, Social, Political, Cultural – which can be learned, and which are important in developing positive and effective relationships at work

Any in-depth understanding about relationships requires an understanding of Emotional Intelligence,[2] that is, the capacity to be aware of and manage our emotions. An increasing awareness of our own emotions and how to manage them helps us also to be aware of the emotional

---

[2] To find out more about Emotional Intelligence, a must-read is Daniel Goleman's book *Emotional Intelligence: why it can matter more than IQ*, Bloomsbury Publishing, 1996.

state of other individuals and groups and so handle interpersonal relationships empathically.

We would expect a person with a high level of Emotional Intelligence as well as technical competence to be successful at work. Familiar sayings like 'We do business with people we like' and 'People buy people first, products and services second' are true – the feeling of rapport, sense of connection and gut intuition that this person is trustworthy happens first – then and only then do we proceed to action. The person who can manage their emotions – and whose behaviour with colleagues is therefore consistent and predictable – inspires a sense of trust, safety and security among their colleagues. Unsurprisingly we tend to shy away from people who seem to value us only for the function that we perform, like some cog in the machine of the organisation, or whose behaviour appears to be unpredictable, irrational or volatile.

The importance of Emotional Intelligence (EQ) as a predictor of professional success has been known for at least 20 years. However, some organisations still promote people based mainly on their technical skills, with relationship skills given secondary consideration, only to discover later just how crucially important these skills are!

At its simplest, the journey of developing one's own EQ flows through four stages:

Stage 2	Stage 3
SELF-ADJUSTMENT *Increasing your ability to control (not suppress) your emotions that are likely to be unhelpful in the situation you are facing.*	*BEING AWARE OF OTHER PEOPLE'S EMOTIONAL STATES* *Becoming increasingly observant of the changes in the emotional states of individuals and groups with whom you interact.*

Stage 1 *SELF-ASSESSMENT* *Ability to become increasingly aware of changes in your own emotional state.*	**Stage 4** *MANAGING AND ADJUSTING YOUR OWN EMOTIONS* *Managing and adjusting your own emotions to match those of others.* *Learning how to use your own emotional states to work for you and not against you by e.g. becoming calm instead of over-anxious, or being empathic, centred and resourceful with a client/colleague who is angry.*

Understanding others starts with understanding oneself

With EQ, like any other personal development skill, it is best to start by working on yourself, i.e. stages 1 and 2 above, before focusing on other people.

Pause for reflection

We've now introduced you to some of the main themes that will recur in this book. Before we introduce other foundational topics, take some time to think about what you would like to take away from this chapter.

Conclusion

In this chapter we've talked about the importance of being intentional about building good relationships at work. Of course, a team that works well together performs well and gets great results, but don't make that your starting point – that's putting the cart before the horse! Start by knowing that your interpersonal skills, and your talent for bringing people together to work collaboratively in mutual respect and understanding, will enable you and your colleagues to be the best that you can be – and *that*, combined with your technical know-how in your field, is what gets results.

If you have spent most of your career so far working hard to develop the essential technical expertise, knowledge and experience you need to flourish, that's great. Now is a good time to realise the full potential of your other, 'people', skills – and if they need sharpening up a little bit, we can help with that – just read on...

Applying this to your workplace

a) Different dimensions of relationships. Look again at the four dimensions of relationships (above). Which dimension(s) do you find it easier to work with? Whilst reading this book we invite you to discover strategies to enable you to work more easily with people in other dimensions

b) Relationship mind-sets. Look at the table below. Take each line ('continuum') in turn. What is your mind-set or your outlook on life? Where is your natural style? – mark a cross on the line for each aspect. The more honest you are, the more value you will get from this exercise!

What matters to me	....	What matters to you
Suspicious and/or secretive	....	Trusting and open
Talk at	....	Listen to
Blaming others	....	Taking responsibility
Protecting my vulnerability	....	Sharing and involving others

c) Mark the topic(s) where you wish to shift your mind-set(s) to the right. Bear this in mind as you continue reading.

Further references

➤ Anderson, Gretchen, *Mastering collaboration: make working together less painful and more productive*, O'Reilly, 2019

➤ Goleman, Daniel, *Emotional Intelligence: why it can matter more than IQ*, Bloomsbury Publishing, 1996

➤ Hasson, Gill, *Emotional Intelligence Pocketbook: little exercises for an intuitive life*, Capstone, 2017

➤ Webb, Caroline, *How to have a good day: the essential toolkit for a productive day at work and beyond*, Pan, 2017

2

The master builder lays the foundation stone: rapport and trust

Trust is the oil that enables an organisation to function smoothly.

Introduction

Building and maintaining rapport and trust is the foundation stone to good team-working and effective client relations. The absence of rapport and trust can cause stilted conversations, a lack of cooperation and commitment, poor performance and high staff turnover.

Building rapport

Have you ever overheard or taken part in these kinds of conversations?

> *'Brian seems to know absolutely everyone in this organisation. How does he find the time?! – For myself I'm too busy just getting on with the job.'*

'My manager, Narisha, has this habit of giving me work without showing any interest in me as a human being – if she even knew my name it would help, but to her I'm just a task-processing robot!'

The first step in creating effective working relationships with colleagues and clients is the ability to build rapport. This means getting to know your work colleagues as human beings rather than simply as functions in the organisation.

You can probably think of certain individuals with whom you felt an instant connection, right from the first meeting – almost as though you had known them for years. Did you hit it off instantly because they had a similar background and interests to yours, or was it because they approached you in an open, friendly way and took a genuine interest in getting to know you?

Rapport is about emphasising the common ground between people and minimising differences. We tend to move towards people who are like us – like attracts like. However, in the workplace we are likely to be working alongside people who have totally different outlooks on life from our own. For these relationships to be effective we need to invest more time and care in building the relationships.

Social intelligence

Daniel Goleman,[1] in his work on social intelligence, describes rapport as a sense of connection or 'attunement'. Intelligence Quotient (IQ) can't be learned but Social Intelligence (SQ) can be enhanced through our experiences with people in a range of social settings.

Learning from our successes and failures, we have all accumulated skills which enable us to navigate different

---

[1] Daniel Goleman, *Emotional Intelligence: why it can matter more than IQ*, Bloomsbury, 1996; and *Social Intelligence*, Arrow Books, 2007.

kinds of social situations effectively. These skills include verbal and conversational skills; an ability to pick up on the informal rules or 'norms' of social interaction; the ability to listen, to be empathic, to play different social roles so that we can feel comfortable with different types of people. At work, an important aspect of social intelligence is the ability to maintain the delicate balance between maintaining a 'professional face' and being authentic in our relationships with others.

We can say that rapport is the *demonstration* of social intelligence. Some people have a natural gift for building rapport, and they are particularly good at three things – small talk, harmonising body language and mirroring choice of words and eye movements. Below is a brief introduction to each.

'Small talk'

At a basic level small talk is about recognising and acknowledging the other person as a fellow human being and taking a keen interest in them. It is important that you are genuinely interested in the other person and that you do not go through some mechanistic routine before getting down to the real work.

Typical topics are sport, local events and places, a major TV series, traffic congestion and, particularly with the British, the weather! You can often ask questions about an object you notice in the other person's workspace, e.g. a photograph of a beautiful landscape or a recent award certificate. Over time you learn how to choose safe topics for this kind of conversation – you may even remember being forewarned in your first job – 'no politics or religion!'

If you find small talk difficult, learn from your colleagues who excel at this. Remember the type of questions they ask and notice how it makes the following business conversation easier.

It is also a great asset if you can acquire the skill of remembering people's names – as Dale Carnegie said, 'Everyone's favourite word is their name.'

There are three other specific skills that can help you enter and stay in rapport with another person. Using these skills will increase your effectiveness as a communicator. These skills are:

> ➢ noticing the other person's body language

> ➢ observing and monitoring their choice of words

> ➢ observing their eye movements

Noticing the other person's body language

When you are with another person with whom you want to build or rebuild rapport it is helpful if your body posture is broadly similar to theirs. Take care not to immediately change your posture each time they change theirs or exactly mirror what you see in front of you. Instead, when your colleague changes position, pause for a few seconds and adopt a broadly similar posture.

You can easily break rapport if your body language is not congruent with what you or the other person are saying. For example, looking over someone's shoulder in the hope of catching the eye of someone else sends a very loud message to the person in front of you that they are not important to you. As a result, when presented with a choice, the other person will tend to believe your body language rather than your words.

Observing and monitoring their choice of words

Each one of us has our unique set of personal preferences in the way we work, think, learn, influence and motivate ourselves. Each of us tends to select different words and phrases when we speak. Your communication will be more effective if you use the same type of words as the other person.

Observing their eye movements

Another clue as to the other person's preferred choice of words is to observe their eye movements whilst they are talking or thinking.

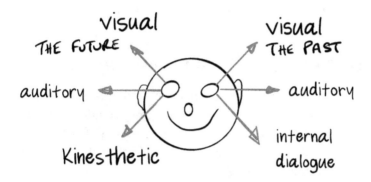

visual
THE FUTURE

visual
THE PAST

auditory

auditory

Kinesthetic

internal
dialogue

Observing eye accessing cues. First postulated in Bandler and Grinder's Frogs into Princes (1979) and widely quoted elsewhere since then

These eye movements, whilst not 100% accurate, give you clues as to the choice of words you could use to keep in rapport and improve the ease of communication.

For a fuller explanation of monitoring another person's body language, their choice of words and their eye movements see the link at the end of this chapter.

Rapport is all about entering the other person's mental map of the world, their reality and matching (or 'pacing') their language preferences, energy levels and non-verbal cues. You continue to pace the other person and listen empathically until you sense that they are ready to move towards listening to your view of the world. Then together you can create a new reality, e.g. 'Let's accept that we have lost this client and recognise we now have time to market our product elsewhere. How do you feel about that?'

Establishing rapport is about setting the tone for the relationship, so the first few moments can be defining moments for the relationship. A combination of verbal and non-verbal communication creates a mood of sociability, openness and warmth which leads to trust. We will say more about non-verbal communication in Chapter 5.

Can I trust you – can you trust me?

This section identifies the main ingredients of trust and why trust is an essential component in good working relationships. We'll give you some examples of behaviours that can damage trust and ways in which you can restore trust if things go wrong.

Pause for reflection

Just take a moment to think of three or four people in your team or department. Which of these colleagues do you trust?

Is there a colleague you do not trust?

What are the ingredients in the relationships with people you trust that are missing with those you mistrust?

How might your behaviour towards other people affect the level of trust between you and others?

What do we mean by trust?

A dictionary definition describes trust as a 'firm belief in the reliability, truth or ability of someone or something'.[2]

---

[2] *Collins Concise English Dictionary*

As most 'beliefs' are emotionally held opinions rather than scientific facts, they are necessarily subjective, and yet these emotional opinions are firmly held. Other people may have different, firmly held opinions about the same situation. You may trust your vintage car to take you and your family 250 km to your holiday destination, whereas your friends would not trust your car and would consider this reckless and foolish. Similarly, with people. You might not trust a person in your team whilst other colleagues seem to be comfortable with having this person as a team member. Often people talk of having a good 'gut feeling' about someone without immediately being able to pin down what it is that has inspired that positive response.

Trust can flourish in teams where shared values – such as honesty, respect, fairness – mean that colleagues honour their explicit and implicit commitments without seeking to take advantage of or undermine other members of the team. We say more about values in Chapter 7.

Team members who trust each other operate more effectively by working more collaboratively – sharing knowledge and experience, trying out new ideas, even taking risks when appropriate – and not being afraid to fail. When they make mistakes, they admit them and learn from them rather than seek to accuse or blame others.

To know more about where trust comes from – and therefore how to build trust – we need to explore beyond the realms of gut feelings and beliefs. But first let's look at the different levels of trust.

Three levels of trust

Trust occurs at three levels:

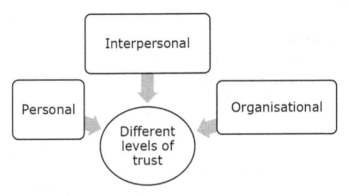

Three levels of trust in an organisation

1. Personal trustworthiness

This refers to private commitments that you either meet or break. For example, 'This afternoon I'm determined to complete that report.' Whether you are the sort of person who carries out your personal commitments determines your level of personal trustworthiness.

If you say only what you genuinely believe, act with integrity and honour your values, you will have a good feeling about yourself and your actions. Your inner satisfaction and consistency of action will in turn enable others to believe in you and trust you.

2. Interpersonal trust

This is the degree of trust between you and each of your colleagues. This will be affected by the quality of your own interpersonal trust. For example, if the mistake you hid came into the open or the report you failed to complete resulted in a missed deadline, these failures – due to dishonesty or secrecy – will cause colleagues to believe that you can't be trusted.

In a closely-knit team, trust is the confidence among the team members that their intentions towards other team members are good and that there is no reason to be protective or overly careful around the group. In essence, team members can be comfortable about being vulnerable with one another. Vulnerability has everything to do with being honest and open about who we are – including our faults, weaknesses, mistakes and limitations. That doesn't mean making yourself vulnerable by over-sharing personal information, but rather being prepared to take full responsibility for the consequences of your own actions and admitting when you do not know the answer to a problem.

How long does it take for team members to trust one another? That depends on the energy, commitment and effectiveness of the team members – people like you! – and on the choices team members decide to make. Here are some common features to look out for as evidence that team members trust each other. They:

➢ ask for help and advice

➢ give and receive feedback

➢ are happy to answer questions about their work

➢ focus on the work that needs to be done

➢ avoid 'bad mouthing' colleagues behind their backs

➢ admit their mistakes and offer to correct them

➢ offer assistance without being asked

➢ enjoy working collaboratively

3. Organisational trust

If organisational trust is high, communication seems to be easy and important information can be shared across the organisation. On the other hand, there could be a general lack of trust throughout the organisation. Signs of this might be a dysfunctional board of directors, a highly political culture, back-stabbing, people climbing over each other to get noticed or promoted, a few toxic relationships that have infected the whole organisation, mixed messages from the directors, or organisational values that have been broken.

A loss of organisational trust is one of the main reasons why employees leave an organisation, or why there is a loss of market share, a fall in the reputation of the company or organisation, or the value of its brand.

However, trust cannot be imposed – it is voluntary and involves accepting a certain degree of vulnerability as you open yourself to being authentic in the relationship. On the other hand, trust assumes that the other's actions will not be harmful to us – or at least not intentionally; trust means that we are willing to be open, to listen, to believe or to be persuaded. Some people set the trust bar very high – and in doing so, they may risk shutting themselves off from colleagues; others will set the bar very low – they need to be careful not to make themselves vulnerable by trusting too early.

Common misconceptions about trust

It is a commonly held opinion that it takes a long time to build trust, but what about if the composition of the team is not fixed over a period of time – because of changing shift patterns, monthly rotas, and the moving around of staff for training purposes – as is the case for healthcare professionals working in hospitals or those who work in the emergency services? In these work environments it is critical to have trust in your colleagues almost immediately if you are to get the job done.

Our experiences and the widespread use of virtual or dispersed teams also dispel the myth that you can only trust someone if you have first met them face to face. Although it may well be easier, it is not an imperative – we will talk more about this in Chapter 13.

Perhaps a more useful belief is 'trust begets trust'. For example, when you place your trust in someone who has been recommended to you by a colleague or friend, you will trust that person to do an excellent job and if, as is likely, they produce an excellent job, this vindicates the trust you have placed in them.

The ingredients of trust

Having built rapport with people, what goes through your mind when you are wondering if you can trust them? When we have raised this question with workshop participants, they have come up with three main factors: the team member's character, their reliability and their credibility.

Character	Reliability
Is the colleague secretive; do they have a hidden agenda? Do they admit mistakes or try to hide them? Do they talk behind other people's backs? Are they likely to take all the credit for a good job or put any blame onto me?	What is their reputation for being reliable? Do they consistently work well and on time? Have they become complacent? Do they take on too much work?

Would I feel safe and secure with them? How are they likely to take feedback from me? Is there something about this person's private life causing me not to trust them?	In short, can I rely on them to complete this task on time, to our agreed standard and within budget?

Credibility

> Roel and I joined the team on the same day. We have very similar educational backgrounds and the same professional qualification, yet he seems to be given the best jobs. A colleague said to me that once you join the company managers quickly forget what is on your CV, but how do I remind my manager of my skills and experience without sounding needy or arrogant?

Seen through the other person's eyes, credibility means 'Do I have the evidence, and am I sufficiently convinced, that you can do this job or that you will be a good representative of our organisation when you meet potential clients?'

Because your managers soon forget what is in your CV, never make the mistake of taking it for granted that your credibility will be known and recognised. You may need to improve your visibility in the team or organisation and find ways of reminding people of your capabilities so that you are not overlooked when interesting opportunities come along.

Your credibility or lack of it is likely to be particularly relevant when meeting clients or other people from outside your organisation. Examples of the evidence you can provide to demonstrate your credibility include:

> your knowledge of their industry sector or field

> your relevant educational attainments and professional qualifications

> the reputation of your current organisation and your previous employer

> without disclosing their names, the types of clients you have worked with and the size and complexity of the projects

> your job title and, if you have a (project) management role, the size of your team

> your prior experience in the type of assignment you would like to undertake

> any publications you have written or external lectures you have given to demonstrate your expertise

> your CV and the social media groups to which you belong (check the content is well-written and up to date)

> your active participation in your social media groups and in contributing to your organisation's technical newsletters, or the local branch of your professional organisation

How trust can get broken

Trust arrives on foot and departs on horseback.
(Chinese proverb)

Trust needs maintenance, just like a building. Without paying attention to the upkeep, fissures and cracks can begin to appear. Here are some examples of ways in which trust can be undermined or broken:

Character	Disclosing information you were told was strictly confidential
	Being aloof and detached from your colleagues
	Not sharing information that would be useful to your colleagues
	Being dishonest, e.g. with expense claims or in your private life
Reliability	Letting people down by only partially completing a task
	Becoming complacent and not as dependable as you used to be
	Bringing personal problems into work and consistently letting them affect your work and/or your colleagues' work
Credibility	Overstating your knowledge or capabilities
	Holding yourself out to be of higher status than your job title

All these problems become magnified when individuals in a team fall into a similar pattern of behaviour – for example, they get into the habit of talking behind people's backs or being secretive.

A breakdown of organisational trust weighs the organisation down. Procedures and processes tend to become more formalised. Without trust, individuals are less inclined to share information and will often try to work more independently in order to have maximum control over their area of responsibility. Lack of cooperation and sharing of information can lead to duplication of effort and work, so that time is wasted. This increase in individual workload – and the formalised and informal checking of colleagues' work – slows down the overall productivity of the organisation. Time and energy are diverted into unproductive 'political' activity and unhelpful behaviours ranging from defensiveness and gossip through to backbiting, blaming and feuding. Such organisations are uncomfortable and stressful places to work in – and often the by-products can be a lower quality of customer service, a drop in profitability and high staff turnover.

When trust is broken – can you repair it?

Trust is the foundation stone of any relationship – the building block on which the stability of the relationship depends – but we are human and there will be occasions when we make a mistake or accidentally let someone down. When trust is broken it can feel like the damage is irreparable – but is there any chance of rescuing the relationship?

Whether trust can be rebuilt depends on several factors:

➢ The organisation's attitude towards mistakes. A few organisations that are serious about innovation or learning may treat most 'mistakes' as feedback and an opportunity for learning, but sadly such organisations are rare

➢ The existing level of trust between you and the other person. If there was a high level of trust between you and a colleague, forgiveness may come quickly. On the other hand, if the level of trust was already low or if you have let down the other person in a serious way then it may take months for trust to be restored, if it ever is

> ➤ The other person's beliefs and values; some people are quick to 'forgive and forget', others will remember the sense of loss for months, if not years

Whilst you can't change other people, you can decide how you are going to handle your mistake or failure and this will influence how well and how quickly trust is restored. Paradoxically, if handled well, it might result in a higher level of trust than before. Some people make the mistake of thinking that you can talk yourself out of a breach of trust. This usually does not work. Actions speak louder than words: for example, immediately admitting to your mistake and undertaking to redo the work in your own time.

Teasing out the above thoughts, you may find the following process useful:

1. Apologise profusely and admit in full that what you did was wrong.

2. Explain who has been or is likely to be affected by this error.

3. Suggest what needs to be done to put the matter right and your willingness to remedy the situation yourself.

4. Acknowledge that this has also potentially damaged the level of trust between you and your colleagues and say what you propose to do in future to restore that trust.

Pause for reflection

Do you have a relationship where the level of trust is low or broken?

What steps could you take to restore the relationship?

Conclusion

For a team to perform well and for an enjoyable workplace, the level of rapport and trust between colleagues needs to be high, particularly if you have a heavy workload with tight deadlines. Building trust takes time and effort. It requires open, honest and transparent communication as well as compassion, kindness, patience and forgiveness of others. It also requires that all the members of the team work collaboratively, agreeing joint goals, and working interdependently to achieve them.

Bear in mind that you do not need to trust your colleagues 100%. It is not as if you are putting your life in their hands. So, if you set the level of trust at 100% before you would entrust your life to someone else, you can set lower levels of trust for your colleagues.

Finally, trust means creating a safe environment in which everyone is free to speak without fear, knowing that they will be heard. This may sometimes mean sharing uncomfortable truths for the sake of continuous improvement and cooperative problem-solving to achieve the shared purpose. Building good team-working relationships depends entirely on the choices that team members decide to make. Hopefully, by reading this book you have decided to opt in to do your part to make your team the best it can be.

Applying this to your workplace

a) Jot down the names of the people you work with most closely, including your manager and your key (internal) clients. What is your level of rapport and trust with each person? How might you improve the situation further?

b) What limited risks could you take to disclose more information about your work and personal life to the colleagues with whom you work most closely?

c) How would you assess your level of credibility with your senior leadership team and with key clients? If you feel that the level needs to be increased, which of our tips are likely to be most useful to you?

d) There are four useful resources in www.learning corporation.co.uk/Library that you are invited to use:

> 'Your preferred choice of words'. This exercise will help you identify your most/least preferred choices of words. Practising your least preferred words will assist you in communicating with your colleagues and clients in ways that they can hear

> A fuller description of building rapport by observing the other person's body language, choice of words and their eye movements

> The Johari Window – try this for yourself

> 'What factors help us trust people in our team?'

Further references

> Apps, Judy, *The art of conversation*, Capstone, 2014

> Blanchard, Ken, Olmstead, Cynthia and Lawrence, Martha, *Trust works! Four keys to building lasting relationships*, HarperCollins, 2013

> Fine, Daniel, *The small talk guidebook: master the unwritten code of social skills*, independently published, 2019

➢ Knight, Sue, *NLP at work – the essence of excellence*, Nicholas Brealey, 2009

➢ Kouzes, James and Posner, Barry, *Credibility: how leaders gain and lose it, why people demand it*, 2nd edition, John Wiley & Sons, 2011

3

Is it just me? Working with different personalities

Introduction

You don't need a doctorate in anthropology or any other 'ology' to realise that each person is unique. We look different, have unique fingerprints, and parts of our eyes and ear lobes are unique too. After working with the same people for a few weeks you start noticing differences in how each person goes about their work, and some differences can be quite prominent.

If you do not realise why each person behaves differently, it can result in misunderstanding and conflict. On the other hand, if you gain some knowledge about diversity or at least become non-judgemental about people's personal preferences, you soon realise that by valuing these differences your team can become more creative, better at exploring opportunities and smarter in solving business problems, because you and your colleagues will be approaching topics from different angles. For example, at a research station a team of very similar personalities was unable to solve an ongoing problem. It wasn't until they recruited a very different personality that, over a few weeks, they were able to permanently sort out their important production issue.

Understanding the preferred ways in which people approach new challenges and learning opportunities can be useful for improving personal and team learning, relationships, your choice of words when you communicate, developing training workshops and client proposals, and studying for professional examinations.

Understanding and working productively with difference is so crucial that we have devoted several chapters to it. In Chapter 4 we look at differences in mind-sets. In Chapter 8 we touch on people's different attitudes towards change; in Chapter 9 the different ways people feel motivated. Chapter 10 talks about identifying individual strengths, and in Chapter 15 we have a more detailed look at cultural differences.

In this chapter we start the process by exploring a small number of commonly used psychometric tests and other tools which assess personality differences. You can relax as none of them are a measure of intelligence or competence. We could have included other types of test, but our aim is to just give you a flavour of the many ways our unique personalities show up at work.

How do you like to learn?

The cycle of learning and learning styles

In the 1970s and 1980s David Kolb, an educationalist at Harvard, developed the concept of the Learning Cycle and Learning Styles. He proposed that for learning to be complete, an individual (and this also applies to team-working) should go through four stages:

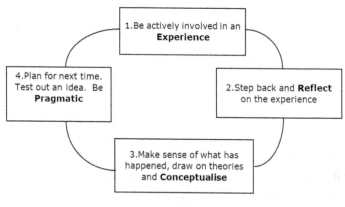

Learning Cycle

In the 1970s and 1980s two UK educationalists, Peter Honey and Alan Mumford, drew on David Kolb's work and developed their own Learning Style model and Learning Styles Questionnaire. Since then they have deepened and widened their areas of research.[1] The terms they used to describe the four steps in the Learning Cycle are: 1. Activist, 2. Reflector, 3. Theorist, and 4. Pragmatist.

Here are the types of behaviours you might observe for each learning style:

An Activist's learning style is to jump straight into action and learn by doing and then move straight on to the next task

A Reflector prefers to hold back, letting others take the lead, before engaging with the topic or speaking at a meeting

---

[1] http://www.peterhoney.org/articles/who-are-honeymumford/

A Theorist's preferred learning style is to first understand the background concepts and framework

A Pragmatist's preference is first to be satisfied on the usefulness of the topic or task to themselves, the organisation and/or clients

A case study illustrating the four learning styles is available at www.learningcorporation.co.uk/Library.

In your day-to-day work it is probable that you, like most other people, have one or perhaps two styles that are more dominant than the others. As a result, you are likely to use these learning styles in preference to others and you may completely overlook your less preferred styles.

In most commercial organisations it seems that Activists are more highly regarded and rewarded than people with a preference as Reflectors, or Theorists or Pragmatists, because they are usually more visible being proactive and 'doing things'. Think about your behaviour and that of your colleagues at team meetings. Is it always the same person who speaks first or jumps up to write on the whiteboard? Do the same people hold back, even though you are sure that they could make a valuable contribution to the meeting? Are all four styles properly represented at the meeting? Perhaps you all project the same strong preference, like a sales team we worked with who all had a strong preference as Activists.

Pause for reflection

What is your usual approach to a new task? How might your personal learning be enhanced by consciously spending more time on your less preferred styles?

What about your team? Does it seem to have a strong preference for one style? If so, how might the team compensate for the weaker preferences?

Each style is valuable and teams as well as individuals need to work through all four styles for learning to be complete.[2]

Keeping a 'lessons learned' or learning journal

Do you and/or your team routinely stop and reflect on the lessons learned from a completed piece of work or a particularly (un)successful presentation or meeting? If not, we suggest you complete the following pro forma at least once a week. It is based on the above four learning styles.

What happened? The experience (Activity)	What do I/we conclude from this? (Reflection)	What do I/we need to be or do differently next time? (Further research and planning)
Experience #1		
Experience #2		

The concept of multiple intelligences

We are all aware of the importance of continuous learning at the personal, team and organisational levels. In a business environment, learning faster is the main way your organisation can maintain its advantage over the competition. One way for continuous learning to become easier and more enjoyable is to discover your preferred ways of assimilating information. Dr Howard Gardner[3] suggested that the traditional notion of intelligence, based on IQ testing, was over-emphasised, and typically seen as more valuable than other 'intelligences'. His main argument is that

---

[2] D. A. Kolb, *The cycle of learning*, McBer, 1985.
[3] Howard Gardner, *Intelligence reframed: multiple intelligences for the 21st century*, Basic Books, 2000.

IQ tests focus mainly on linguistic and logical-mathematical abilities, and that the broad scope of other inherent mental abilities should be recognised. He therefore proposed seven different intelligences (later expanded to nine) to account for a broader range of human potential and which could be used to engage with the learning process.

Intelligence	Some characteristics	What you might hear
Kinesthetic	Learns through the fingertips and by being hands-on; 'muscle memory'.	My interest in engineering started with my first Meccano set when I was seven. Please pass that gadget to me.
Visual/spatial	Likes 'big pictures', diagrams, mind-maps and uncluttered graphs.	Let's put this together in a diagram. This picture communicates what we want to get across.
Interpersonal	Likes human contact, sensitive to other people's moods and feelings.	Let's talk this through at our next meeting. I would prefer to meet rather than correspond by email.
Intra-personal	A satisfactory team member who prefers to learn alone.	I will take this document away and study it quietly.

Musical	Sensitive to sounds and background music!	Let's work with the rhythm of this change programme.
Verbal/ linguistic	Likes reading, writing and listening to good speakers.	I find mnemonics a useful aid to memory.
Logical/ mathematical	Likes to be systematic and able to break down challenges into logical steps.	What's the reasoning behind your proposal? Can I see the statistics?

Implications for learning and working relationships

➤ Although you can access all these intelligences, two or three of them are likely to stand out as your strong preferences

➤ You tend to communicate with others out of your strongest preference. But just because you prefer diagrams and pictures don't assume that this will engage other members of your team or your clients. The quotation by Fred Barnard, 'A picture is worth a thousand words', is not, by any means, true for everyone. The tip when communicating is to vary the range of intelligences you use

➤ There is a danger of assuming that members of the same profession share the same top preference. For example, verbal/linguistic may not be the strongest preference with lawyers and we clearly remember working with a global team of qualified accountants where logical/mathematical was, on average, their third highest preference

➢ Starting with your own preferred route to learning can be the most effective way to engage and motivate yourself in learning new information. For a deeper understanding you then need to use other intelligences

➢ Your colleagues and clients may give you clues about their preferred intelligences by the words and phrases they use and their favourite pastimes

➢ It is so easy to be engaged in a 'violent agreement' with a colleague when you are both essentially meaning the same thing but one of you is talking from, e.g. a visual/spatial preference using big-picture, visual terms whilst the other person is thinking and speaking chronologically step by step, or in concrete terms, or expressing their feelings

Our preferred ways of assimilating and then communicating information

There have been several occasions in our careers when we have been engaged by organisations specifically to help them improve the way they share learning with their staff and with clients. Here is a brief summary of one example.

A science-based organisation sold products to farmers and horticulturalists. The company employed scientists and the sales team organised seminars for their major customers with the aim of persuading them to purchase the company's products. These seminars were a failure. We asked how these seminars had been delivered. They showed us their slide presentation – a collection of extremely 'busy' slides each one packed with words, figures, tables and colour (most PowerPoint slides that organisations produce have little Power and no Point!). The staff also showed us the manuals they handed out which were full of technical information.

We asked our client to describe how farmers and horticulturalists learn about the condition of their soil, their crops and other produce. They said that they were very practical people and would, for example, feel the wheat to see if it was ready to be harvested and would check on the condition of the soil by running a handful of soil through their fingers. It seemed that the farmers' preferred way of taking in new information was kinesthetic – learning by touching and handling. Their second preference was using their sight – a visual/spatial preference. They also enjoyed opportunities to meet each other and discuss topics of mutual interest (interpersonal learning).

At future client presentations our client left their slide presentation and manuals in the office and instead handed out to each participant a tin or bottle of the product they wanted to discuss. The labels on each product explained in pictures and in words the composition of the product, how it should be applied, and safety warnings. It was a much more successful learning and sales event.

If you would like to learn more about your own preferred multiple intelligences, there is a link at the end of this chapter.

Are you task-focused or people-focused; a fast thinker and worker or more measured and slower-paced?

Have a look at the following four styles of working. What style best describes you? As with other personality types we cover there is no 'correct, textbook answer' nor is one preference better or worse than the others. However, a strong preference for one of the types has its own positive and negative implications.

Style 1	*Style 2*
Sociable, fun-loving, easy communicator, energetic, enjoys being with colleagues, talkative, easily bored, a joker who may not be taken seriously	Personable, everyone seems to like this person, caring and considerate, patient and tolerant, people come before business, happy to act as no. 2 in team, encourager of others
Style 3	*Style 4*
Thrives on goals and targets, a quick thinker, task-focused, may be insensitive to, or dominate, other people, a 'driven' person, happy to take a leadership role, can be impatient with others	Operation, process and task-orientated, thorough, perfectionist, prefers structure and clear procedures, thinks through issues carefully and worries about doing tasks incorrectly, not a great lover of change, risk or making big decisions

As with similar exercises, when you look at a style which broadly describes you, don't expect to identify with every characteristic of that one style. You are likely to be a mix of two or perhaps three styles, of which one style is likely to be dominant.

If you conclude that, on balance, your dominant style is either 1 or 2 above, you are likely to be a people-focused person. If 3 or 4 then a task-focused person. If you are in category 1 or 3 then you are likely to be a fast thinker and completer of tasks. A category 2 or 4 style suggests you tend to work in a more measured, slower way than colleagues in categories 1 and 3.

Implications regarding working relationships

➢ Take your own preferred style and imagine you are working with a colleague with a diametrically opposite style. If you are under a lot of stress, what might cause difficulties, even conflict between you? Who would do most of the talking to the client or to the line manager? Would the other person be happy to always be in the background?

➢ Knowing that we tend to recruit like-minded people, let's assume that you and the other members of your small team all prefer the same style. When you are working together what topics are you in danger of overlooking?

Two people, with different working styles, if they respect and trust each other, can make an effective double act by combining their complementary preferred working styles and capabilities.

If you would like to pursue this further, you might care to look at, for example, www.insights.com.

What is your informal role at work?

Have you noticed a team member who is good at coming up with fresh ideas or another team member who starts things up, but who is not good at following them through to completion? Or have you experienced a colleague who is very methodical and can spot errors in the team's work, or another colleague who is diplomatic and a good listener and can keep things running smoothly? These are what is meant by taking on an 'informal role'.

In the 1970s Dr Meredith Belbin studied many different types of teams. He observed the behaviour of individual team members and noticed how team workers adopted informal roles depending on their personal preferences. Belbin concluded that for teams to perform well the team members should cover a wide range of informal roles. When he first published his research on team roles,[4] he originally stated that there were eight major informal roles, for example Completer Finisher, Resource Investigator and Monitor Evaluator. He later added a ninth role, Expert or Specialist.

Belbin created a Team Role Inventory which has been used by many teams to help them, first, to become aware of their strengths and weaknesses in these nine roles, and secondly, to discuss how they might improve their performance by role-playing any missing or weak roles.

You can find out more about Meredith Belbin and his team roles at www.belbin.com.

---

[4] M. Belbin, *Management teams: why they succeed or fail*, Heinemann, 1981.

Carl Jung and Myers Briggs

Many of the psychometric tools in use today are based on the work of the famous psychoanalyst Carl Jung. He developed some interesting ideas about personality 'type' and the concept of 'preferences', which were popularised by Katharine Briggs and her daughter Isabel Briggs Myers. In the 1940s they devised a psychometric tool known as the Myers-Briggs Type Indicator (MBTI).[5]

Briefly, 'type' can be defined as an underlying preference for the way we act, a personality pattern that is innate, but influenced by the environment and our own choices.

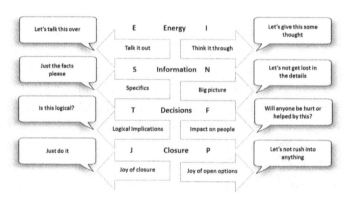

The eight major thought processes of the MBTI

As illustrated above, the MBTI tool is based on the following four pairings:

Extravert (E) and Introvert (I)

Sensing (S) and Intuition (N)

Thinking (T) and Feeling (F)

Judging (J) and Perceiving (P)

---

[5] The Myers Briggs Foundation, www.myersbriggs.org.

MBTI terms like 'Introvert', 'Sensing' and 'Judging' have specific meanings which differ from those used in everyday life.

We do not want to give the impression that with each of the pairings, e.g. 'Thinking' and 'Feeling', you are wholly one or the other. Everyone can use all 16 type preferences, though not at the same time, but usually you would show as having a mild or strong preference for one or the other. If you have a particularly strong preference for one or more of the types, your challenge is to moderate your behaviour so you can work more smoothly with your clients and colleagues.

If your work demands that you spend a lot of time in a type that is clearly not your preferred style, this will cause you extra effort and over the long term could be stressful. For example, over the years we have witnessed several occasions where HR directors have been uncomfortable in their job role because, in order to 'fit in' with the other board directors, they have behaved in ways that were not their natural style.

MBTI is one of the deepest and most well-researched personality inventories, which can help you understand yourself and others. The MBTI feedback report can help you become more aware of the implications of your own preferences and can form a useful basis for improving your personal effectiveness and your working relationships with colleagues.

DISC

There are countless other psychometric tests, of which probably the most well-known is DISC. This was developed by the inventor of the lie detector, William Moulton Marston, and honed by industrial psychologist Walter Clark. It began to be used in the 1950s and is said to be the most commonly used psychometric tool worldwide today. The DISC profile centres on four different personality traits: Dominance (D), Influence (I), Steadiness (S), and Conscientiousness (C).

The strengths and limitations of psychometric tools

You are not your profile type. You are much, much more than that.

First, let's be clear about language. Psychometric tools are not *tests*; they do not *measure* intelligence, competence, mental stability, or maturity, and the majority give little or no indication of commitment, determination, passion, experience, or ambition. They do not *define* you as a person. Usually, if you are recruiting a person it is preferable to interview them against a detailed job description.

A psychometric tool is about preferences, not skills, and is a snapshot of part of you at a point in time. The way you answer each question may vary depending on whether you are feeling full of energy and enthusiasm or totally exhausted and dejected. Your responses to questions will also vary depending on whether your answers are based on a specific recent good or bad experience or you are answering in general terms. One preference is not inherently 'better' than another and the results do not provide a universal answer to individual or team challenges.

However, these tools can provide the starting point for self-discovery through reflection and learning. Also, in an environment of high trust they offer an opportunity and the language to talk about difference in a non-judgemental way so that team members can work out the effective ways of working together.

Here is a Health and Safety Notice about the use of psychometric tools...

Health and Safety Notice

To a man who has a hammer, everything he encounters begins to look like a nail.

(Mark Twain)

When a person has been certified to use a psychometric or other type of feedback tool, they are likely to be keen to practise using it. The danger is that the tool starts to be used in situations where it is not applicable. For example, the tool may not be designed for use in recruitment, or in deciding who should be promoted. In addition, in a low-trust environment such tools can be used with ulterior motives – for example, to manipulate a situation towards a certain outcome, or to ridicule or undermine individuals in the team, e.g. 'You can't expect her to make a decision, she's a "P"!'

If you are asked to complete a psychometric test you are entitled to ask questions such as:

➤ What are we seeking to achieve by using a psychometric tool?

➤ Is this tool the most appropriate tool to use?

➤ How will I receive feedback on the results of the assessment?

➤ Who else will see my results?

➤ Do these other people appreciate that the tool is about preferences and not about intelligence or competence?

> How will this profiling activity be followed-up and used for further development (my own, or that of the team)?

Be wary of online personality 'tests':

> Know the origins of the theory

> Look on the internet for evidence of solid research and validation of results

> Expect to pay for taking a profiling tool questionnaire based on research: serious research is expensive

> Abbreviated online versions of longer tests can give misleading results

Don't go it alone

Information delivered 'cold' through online questionnaires also can be unhelpful – even destructive. Work through the feedback report with a qualified coach or mentor. During the debriefing a professional will make clear to you the limits of the tool and help you to use what is helpful to you, and discard what does not apply to you.

Trust and confidentiality

Psychometric tools are intended to be confidential. However, if team members trust each other enough to talk openly about their individual differences (and similarities), the positive impact can be considerable.

Conclusion

> It is not the strongest of the species that survives, nor the most intelligent that survives. It is the one most adaptable to change.
>
> (Charles Darwin)

The small sample of tools we have mentioned in this chapter can help you increase your self-awareness, build better relationships and become more effective in your professional life. Today's fast-changing work environment means that everyone is expected to be able to take on a variety of roles, manage high pressure environments, be creative and learn fast – in addition to being knowledgeable and skilled in your own area of professional expertise. Understanding more about yourself and your preferences will also help you to become more aware of ways in which you might enhance your lesser preferences so that you can be even more effective at work.

Navigating your way through the many other psychometric tests and diagnostic tools available can be confusing. Before using any tool, please check the Health and Safety Notice in this chapter and remember:

➢ Preferences should not be confused with intelligence, common sense, skills or competence

➢ You are not limited to the sum of your preferences

➢ No one can 'tell' you who you are, but there are ways of gaining insights that will help you on your journey of self-discovery and greater effectiveness

Psychometric tools are constantly being reviewed and updated to ensure continued relevance and applicability. As neuroscience research progresses, we are gradually understanding even more about the ways in which, despite the physical and neurological similarities in the structure of our brains, each one of us is unique.

Applying this to your workplace

a) If you have any strong preferences, then looking back over the last few weeks, which of these have been:

> - a significant benefit in your day-to-day work and private life; or

> - a cause of disappointment, frustration or conflict?

b) Have any of your lower preferences resulted in under-performance or lack of personal satisfaction? If so, how might you build them up to increase your personal effectiveness as a team player at work?

c) What aspects of personality would you like to explore further to find out more about yourself and your relationships with others?

d) Which of the Team Roles do you typically seem to occupy? What potential development and promotion opportunities might be available to you if you focused on trying out other roles within the team?

e) If you would like to find out more about how to optimise your learning preferences at work, have a look at the Multiple Intelligences Questionnaire, available at www.learningcorporation.co.uk/Library

f) If you find the concept of celebrating diversity a bit of a challenge, we invite you to review a process called the Diversity Awareness Ladder, a copy of which can also be found at www.learningcorporation.co.uk/Library

Further references

- ➢ Belbin, R. Meredith, *Team roles at work*, Routledge, 2010

- ➢ Gardner, Howard, *Multiple intelligences: new horizons in theory and practice*, Basic Books, 2006

- ➢ Kroeger, Otto and Thuesen, Janet M., *Type talk: the 16 personality types that determine how we live, love, and work*, Dell Publishing, 2013

- ➢ Kummerow, Jean M., Barger, Nancy J. and Kirby, Linda K., *Work types: understand your work personality*, Grand Central Publishing, 2010

- ➢ Murden, Fiona, *Defining you: how to profile yourself and unlock your full potential*, Nicholas Brealey, 2018

Mind-sets and relationships

We do not see the world the way it is, we see it the
way we are.

(The Talmud)

Introduction

We briefly introduced the concept of mind-sets at the end
of Chapter 1. Mind-sets, sometimes referred to as 'mental
perceptions', 'paradigms', 'mental frameworks' or 'outlooks
on life', cover all aspects of our lives. Each of us has many
mind-sets on topics like our own capabilities, our line
manager, the market we work in, social media, millennials
and individual colleagues.

Our mind-sets are constructed from a variety of sources
such as our upbringing, environment, beliefs, assumptions,
motivations and personal values. Most of these learnt ways
of being are still valid and useful to us in our relationships.
Others may now be out of date, or incomplete or just plain
wrong.

In this chapter we would like to share with you some of the
ways in which our thinking patterns can affect our behaviour
and our relationships, often in adverse ways, and offer
suggestions for learning alternative, more helpful, mind-sets.

Why mind-sets matter in relationships

One of the greatest barriers to enjoying healthy working relationships and a healthy state of mind is to be trapped by our own thinking. How frequently do you hear comments at work like this: *'I think he's trying to get me moved to another department'; 'She's never liked me'; 'Are you for or against this idea?'*

Most of us have had occasions when a thought – usually a negative one – has been going around and around in our head for several days. Each time this thought pops up in our conscious mind it feels as if it is getting stronger. It doesn't seem to take long before that thought seems as real as any physical barrier and we can feel trapped by it.

It's crazy, isn't it, that a thought which is entirely intangible can put such a physical constraint on our actions and relationships. We invite you to challenge the next person who says, 'This project will end in disaster', before this thought triggers a chain of actions and failure becomes the physical reality. As Mike Dooley[1] says:

Choose them wisely, thoughts become things!

The more you can spot fixed mind-sets in others – and more particularly in yourself – the more you can free up your thinking to discover alternative options and build better relationships. Let's take a look at some of the things we do when we are in a fixed mind-set.

---

[1] M. Dooley, *Choose them wisely: thoughts become things!* Simon & Schuster, 2009.

Mind-sets in action

Put simply, our mind-set is a strong influence on how we behave, and our behaviour generates a satisfactory or an unsatisfactory outcome.

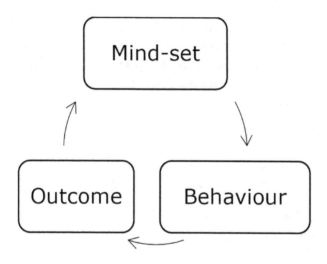

How our mind-sets can determine outcomes

For example, you are asked to meet a potential client whom you have never met before. You think that the market is extremely competitive ('mind-set') so you try hard to secure this client by endeavouring to convince them of the uniqueness of your product ('behaviour'). Later you learn that you have lost this potential client (outcome) because the person felt pressurised and you had not listened to their viewpoint and needs.

When the outcome is satisfactory it tends to reinforce the mind-set, so you will probably repeat the same behaviour on the next occasion. When the outcome is not what you want, you will probably think back to what you did and resolve to try harder next time ('behaviour'). However, is doing more of what you've already done necessarily the answer to achieving the outcome you intended?

If you always do what you've always done, you will always get what you've always got.

(Henry Ford)

Instead of focusing on what you did last time, try reviewing your mind-set – there's a good chance that this was a contributing factor to the unsatisfactory outcome.

You can also add an additional stage, 'Reflect and create a new mind-set':

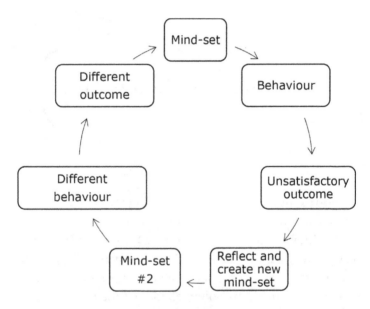

Reflecting on your mind-set to get the outcome you want

Here is an example of when you might decide to reconsider your mind-set. You might say to yourself:

Tudor and I are both team leaders. His workload is like mine yet every day I work, on average, 1.5

hours more than he does. Our line manager seems happy with his work. Perhaps if I adopt his outlook ('mind-set') towards his work, particularly about delegation ('behaviour'), I'll be able to reduce my working hours and have a better work–life balance ('outcome').

Pause for reflection

Do you have a relationship you would like to improve? What change of attitude or perspective (mind-set) could you make which might improve the situation? Is there a particular task you dislike? Again, a change of mind-set could make life more enjoyable.

How mind-sets work – beliefs and assumptions

As mentioned at the beginning of this chapter, key components of our mind-sets are our beliefs and assumptions. We accumulate our set of beliefs, assumptions, attitudes and perspectives from our upbringing, our education and our life experiences. We accept them as true in our lives and the worlds we inhabit, even though they are mostly emotionally held opinions and there may be little or no proof to support them. Because our beliefs and assumptions are real and true for us, the mind-sets that they create may become difficult to shift.

The destructive power of self-limiting beliefs

> Whether you think you can or whether you think you can't, you are right.

> (Henry Ford)

Here are some other examples of self-limiting beliefs. Do you recognise any of these?

- ➤ If you trust people, they will take advantage of you

- ➤ I cannot trust people I have not met

- ➤ I cannot do x because of y, e.g. because I'm new to the team or I'm too young

- ➤ Nothing I say is worth listening to

- ➤ I would prefer to keep quiet at meetings, I don't want to look stupid

- ➤ I don't do change – you can't teach an old dog new tricks

- ➤ I can't change my behaviour, it's just who I am

- ➤ People think I'm boring because I prefer not to be involved in the business development side of the company

- ➤ I'm overworked. I must be incompetent

You will notice that, with most of the above examples, the limiting belief is a mechanism to protect ourselves. But are we being over-protective? Are we generalising (see section below)?

An understanding of neuroscience[2] can help you identify, for example, what is holding you back or preventing you from having a happier and more successful life.

Self-fulfilling prophesies

Certain beliefs and assumptions are close to the core of who we are – so we look for evidence to prove them to ourselves.

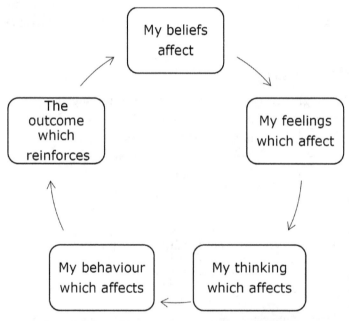

Some beliefs and assumptions can become self-fulfilling

For example. You were asked to make an important presentation to your top management team. You have given presentations before but not to such important people. You kept thinking that you would not make a good impression and you eventually convinced yourself that the presentation

---

[2] Steve Peters, *The Chimp Paradox: the mind management programme to help you achieve success, confidence and happiness*, Random House, 2012.

was likely to be a disaster. On the day of the presentation you were stressed out, you fumbled operating the visual aids, which caused you to have a mild panic, your breathing became shallow and you were told afterwards that you looked nervous and lacked enthusiasm and conviction.

Remember you can change an assumption or belief if you choose to do so. Prove this to yourself by thinking back to a belief you used to have but no longer believe. Think back to the rich mind-sets you had about Father Christmas and the Tooth Fairy!

How to change a belief

Although you can work through the following process by yourself, the exercise may be more effective if you work with a qualified coach or a trusted colleague.

My limiting belief or assumption   What evidence is there for this belief? Is it 100% true or only e.g. 20% true?
What would be an alternative positive or empowering belief?   What acceptable risks could I take to shift my unhelpful self-limiting belief and thereby liberate myself?

Imagine a person with this alternative belief. What sort of things would they feel, say and do?

Can I do or say these things? When and how will I test this new belief or assumption?

Over the coming months continue to focus on the positive results of applying your new belief or assumption in order to stop the old belief re-establishing itself.

Other types of mind-sets: generalising, deleting and distorting

Unconscious mind-sets often manifest themselves in the way we communicate. Habits of generalising, deleting or distorting information can be the vehicle for validating strongly held beliefs and assumptions. These habitual responses, when traced to source, are often about wanting to create a feeling of safety and security. They appear to offer quick answers and easy solutions but are usually inaccurate, serving only to reinforce unhelpful attitudes and sloppy thinking – which then creates 'noise' in interpersonal communications – which has the potential to undermine relationships.

Taking a metaphor from IT, each of the above three mind-sets could be like your personal internal operating system, ticking quietly away in the background influencing the way you think and speak. As well as being unhelpful in relationships, they can also get in the way of our own well-being and happiness, so it's important to look out for these responses – and challenge them when we spot them. Here are some suggestions. First, a colleague who has a tendency to generalise:

Statement	Clarifying questions
He's always doing that. I'm always putting my foot in it.	Always? Every single time?
You can't trust people you have not met.	What stops you? What, not even to do this simple task?
She'll never improve her behaviour.	What particular behaviour are you talking about? What low risk could you take on this project?
It's always been like that and it always will be.	What about the changes that were implemented in February and the one only last week?

A person who has a tendency to delete information omits to mention points that the listener would have expected to hear in order to make the statement clear or more complete:

Statement	Clarifying questions
Bits of the meeting were OK.	Which bits? In what way? What did they discuss during the rest of the meeting?
People are starting to talk.	Who? What are they saying? What evidence do they have?

In other situations, clarifying questions might be 'How precisely?', 'What specifically?', 'In what way?', 'Where exactly?', 'What else?'

Distortion can occur when someone says something that we find difficult to fit into our mental framework of the world. We need to listen and ask questions to make connections between their world and ours:

Statement	Clarifying questions
You're not going to like this!	What exactly? How do you know I won't like it? or What gave you that idea?
It's totally unacceptable.	What is 'it'?
With a laugh like that she must have lots of friends.	That's a new line of thinking for me. What's the connection between her laugh and lots of friends?

| This idea is a definite winner. | Tell me more. How do you know that this idea will work for us/me? |
| They're saying that .... | Who has been saying that? When did they say that? Have you checked with x what they said? |

Building a positive mind-set: win-win thinking

A wonderful attitude for building and maintaining relationships in the workplace, as well as at home, is to have the mind-set of win-win thinking. By win-win thinking we mean that in a dilemma, challenge or difference of opinion you seek a solution that works for both parties. This approach is particularly useful when you are delegating work, giving feedback, in performance review discussions, meetings with clients, or wanting to be creative.

Win-win thinking requires two character traits to be in balance:

➤ treating the other person with respect and listening attentively to their point of view; and then

➤ being assertive when explaining your position and your needs

If you are full of consideration and kindness for others but low on personal courage and/or assertiveness you can end up with lose-win agreements. Over time you can start to feel 'used', become resentful and possibly lose the respect of colleagues for not being able to stand up for yourself. A team member who is extremely friendly and kind may fall into this trap.

On the other hand, if you are over-assertive with little regard for others you will go for a win-lose position in which your aim is to be the winner! While you may 'win' on several occasions, you may find that, over time, your attitude and behaviour creates tension and distrust in the team and some colleagues may keep out of your way. A team member who is extremely ambitious and strives for promotion may fall into this trap.

In order to ensure a win-win outcome for all, invite the other person to speak first and ask them to explain what a win-win outcome would look like for them in a relationship or in completing a task which involves you. You can then:

> reflect back your understanding of what you heard them say; then

> explain what a win-win looks like for you; and

> discuss how you both could achieve a win-win

This win-win mind-set of course requires personal and professional integrity. We have probably all experienced a colleague who works hard to establish win-win relationships with those that they consider to be peers or more senior, but thinks nothing of slipping into 'I win you lose' when working with either a junior colleague, or someone they know to be extremely considerate and helpful.

Breaking free from the prison of 'binary thinking'

Binary thinking, where only two options are presented as being possible, is widespread. This is the temptingly attractive world of either/or thinking in which simplistic arguments and facile solutions often replace careful listening and thinking:

You do it this way or not at all

I'm right and you are wrong

Do you believe in this proposal or not?

Is your answer yes or no?

You'll notice how frequently journalists pressure politicians to respond in this either/or way when common sense tells us the topic is complicated and not 100% one way or the other.

There is a time and a place for binary thinking, for example after a full discussion or sales meeting when it seems an appropriate time to reach a decision. However, if binary thinking is used early in the discussion it can kill creativity, narrow the range of options and lead to conflict. Statements like 'My idea is stronger than yours' can encourage both parties to argue and fight for their corner. A contest begins. Egos become inflated. Each person digs in their heels. The contest becomes the survival of the loudest.

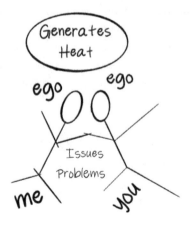

Illustration of binary thinking

As well as intellectual laziness, part of the underlying cause of binary thinking seems to be a combination of pride and a scarcity mentality – that is, a belief that there will never be enough recognition, credit, ideas, power, money to share.

Implications thinking, on the other hand, operates from an abundance mindset and recognises that in many work situations there are more than two ways forward.

An abundance mentality is about being able to let go of the need to defend your own position. It's a belief that there are plenty of resources – creative ideas, praise, recognition, alternatives, potential clients – 'out there' for everybody. It results in sharing possibilities, options, decision-making, prestige, recognition and profits.

When two individuals are in discussion, for implications thinking to flourish two things need to be in place. First, a sufficiently high degree of emotional maturity and trust between the two individuals. Second, a willingness to put the other person first.

It is therefore important that both people do their best to let go of the ownership of their original idea. The objective is to come up with a triple win-win-win, i.e. the best solution for both individuals plus the client or organisation.

Here is a process we have shared with many workshop participants who have later told us that the process worked successfully:

1. Arrange to sit alongside the other person and place your notepad and other paperwork 'out there' on the table in front of both of you. This action, in itself, helps to 'separate the person from the topic' and helps you both to have a more objective discussion.

2. You can invite the other person to act as scribe or better still take it in turns to be scribe.

3. You take it in turns to discuss each other's proposal – Proposals A and B. You both think positively about Proposal A and write down all the positive points without discussing them – positive points in the short term and in the longer term.

4. When you have both exhausted all the positive points about Proposal A you both think and write down all the negative points both in the short term and in the longer term, again without any discussion.

5. You then repeat the exercise for Proposal B.

6. It is important to exhaust all the positive implications before switching to the negative ones (how the brain likes to jump between the two!) and also to defer any discussion and evaluation until the exercise is complete.

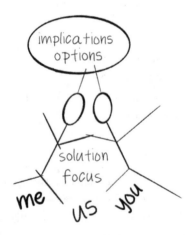

Illustration of implications thinking

7. It is helpful when carrying out this exercise to hold on to the belief that by trusting and respecting each other you will both think of other ideas that neither

of you thought of before the meeting. When this happens, you write down the third or fourth or fifth proposal and repeat the implications thinking exercise for each option.

8. When you both feel that you have exhausted all options you then dispassionately review all the proposals and decide on the most suitable win-win-win proposal to take forward.

Pause for reflection

Think of an opportunity in the near future when you could use the above process with a colleague or client.

Mind-sets about time: past, present and future

> With our thoughts we make the world.
>
> (The Buddha)

There's another set of preferences on thinking that can affect our relationships, and this is to do with our mind-sets regarding time present, time past and time future. In the western world many of us have a preference for either:

➢ living in the past; or

➢ living in the future; or

➢ living in the present

Living in the past

A team member with a strong preference for living in the past may talk frequently about their previous employer or boss, the systems they used and their past achievements.

After a while, you and your colleagues may find this rather tedious and assume that the speaker is not engaged and committed to your organisation.

A strong preference for living in the past can also become a handicap in our fast-changing world where the need to let go of the past is usually a prerequisite for engaging with new ways of thinking and working. For all of us the past is also where thoughts of guilt, resentment, regrets and disappointments thrive. These can hold us prisoner, drain our energy and damage our relationships.

Living in the future

A team member who has a preference for living in the future often has a strong need to think and plan well ahead. Over-using this preference can cause pushback from colleagues when they are asked to put dates in their diaries which are often months, even a year or more ahead. This kind of scheduling might be considered impractical, unrealistic or constricting by others.

A team member with a strong preference for living in the future may see the past as an indistinct blur and have difficulty recalling facts and figures and meetings as recent as a few days ago. Colleagues may regard this apparent loss of memory as a sign of lack of intelligence, or interest, and commitment to the team, organisation or client.

The future is also where thoughts of anxiety, apprehension, fear and stress reside. These thoughts can hold us prisoner and if we keep sharing them with colleagues, they can create a downward spiral of negative thinking which can be de-motivating both for the individual and for the team.

Living in the present

The person who has a strong preference for living in the present moment seems to be rare and sometimes to be envied. Colleagues may both admire and be frustrated by the way in which this person seems to manage not to get caught up in worrying about deadlines or becoming addicted to urgency or to the clock. They meet deadlines but their 'just in time' attitude can cause their line manager and colleagues a lot of stress!

Using the present moment as your base

There has been much talk recently about teaching meditation and mindfulness at work. You may feel that you don't have time to stop what you're doing and be mindful, for example by focusing on your breath. Indeed it does take some practice to sit still and empty your mind of what is bothering it. However, if you can learn to do this (and most people need to go on a short course to learn how), you will find that as you reconnect with being in 'the present', or in 'the now',[3] it's like a reset button for the brain. In the stressful work conditions caused by volume of work and lack of support, meditation and mindfulness can be of real practical help – it's not a cop-out.

Conclusion

In conclusion, you will have realised the significant impact that mind-sets have on our actions. Most of our mind-sets work well for us and do not need to be adjusted. The beauty is that we can change any mind-set that is a barrier to our relationships at work and to our enjoyment and our general well-being. If this chapter has whetted your appetite, we have included several exercises and books in the next sections.

---

[3] E. Tolle, *The power of now,* Mobius, 2001.

Applying this to your workplace

Having read this chapter, which of your thinking preferences or patterns would you like to change to become even more personally effective, to improve your relationships and your emotional well-being?

Questions to help you develop your own action plan:

a) Reflect on feedback you may have had from your manager, a colleague, friends or family. Are you aware of an assumption or a self-limiting or self-fulfilling belief that is holding you back or might be the cause of a potentially difficult relationship? If so, we invite you to complete the exercise in this chapter

b) Do you ever notice generalisations, deletions or distortion in your own interpersonal communication? Try to aim for greater clarity from within by paying attention to the language you use

c) Looking back on discussions with your key relationships, do you generally end up with win-win? If not and the outcome tends to be win-lose or lose-win how might you achieve win-win outcomes instead?

d) When will you have an opportunity to practise implications thinking using the process we have shared with you?

e) Which preference do you have: living in the past, living in the present or living in the future? How might moderating your preference improve your work-life and/or your general well-being?

Further references

➢ Boyd, J. and Zimbardo, P., The time paradox: using the new psychology of time to your advantage, Rider, 2010

➢ Brann, A., *Make your brain work*, Kogan Page, 2013

➢ Doidge, N., *The brain that changes itself*, Penguin, 2007

➢ Fox, R. and Brown, H., *Creating a purposeful life – how to reclaim your life, live more meaningfully and befriend time*, Infinite Ideas Limited, 2012

➢ Meadow, M., *Confidence: how to overcome your limiting beliefs and achieve your goals*, CreateSpace Independent Publishing Platform, 2015

5

Communicating from the inside out

Anneliese Guérin-LeTendre

The problem with communication is the illusion
that it has occurred.

(George Bernard Shaw)

Introduction

As social animals we human beings have spent whole
civilisations trying to work out how we can live and thrive
together – and we're still learning! The degree to which our
communication is successful provides a kind of barometer
indicating our success in this endeavour.[1]

In this chapter I'll be taking a closer look at interpersonal
communications – that is, the process through which we
express feelings, ideas, thoughts, information, attitudes and
emotions in the form of a 'message' – either verbal or non-
verbal. I'll be inviting you to observe these communication

---

[1] The Greek philosopher Aristotle is thought to have proposed
the first 'Linear Model of Communication' before 300 BC!

processes more carefully – and to be more intentional in your own communication.

I'll also be highlighting a few examples of typical roadblocks and distractors which might be getting in the way of you being a top communicator. Some of this troublesome interference appears to arrive out-of-the-blue and out of our control, but in reality a lot of interference is generated by us, the communicators.

We'll be focusing here on spoken communication – written communication presents particular joys and challenges of its own, although there are of course key features common to both. You'll also notice that the skill of listening, vital for all effective communicators, is so important that it has an entire chapter to itself.

Communication is a complex process; as you become more aware of how communication works, you will gain more clarity about your own communication, find it easier to learn from your previous experiences, be better prepared for future interactions, and understand more about the communication among members of your team.

Becoming a skilful communicator

When we think about communication with others we often imagine ourselves going 'out' – pushing our words and ideas into the air where they will be caught and understood by the listener. And yet, communication is a process that has its origins within.

You instinctively know this. You've probably attended excellent interpersonal skills training programmes but still been left wondering why, when you wanted to be assertive, you ended up being bamboozled into doing something you didn't want to do. Perhaps you remember kicking yourself when, yet again, you found yourself taking on more work and responsibility instead of appropriately delegating? Maybe you've recently backed down from a difficult performance feedback conversation. In all cases, I suspect that you weren't short of frameworks and strategies to use and key questions to ask. What held you back was more than likely happening inside your head and heart – anxiety, nervousness, lack of confidence, memories of past experiences – self-defeating limiting beliefs and overpowering emotions which get in the way of your best intentions.

Naturally it takes a while to learn how to use new communications tools – it takes practice for them to sound natural and effortless. Unfortunately, in the rush to sort out communication challenges, there can be a temptation to go straight to the tools without taking the first step of thinking about what's going on for you during the interaction – what you're thinking, what you're feeling, and the range of experiences and learning you bring to that interaction. Unsurprisingly, communication quick fixes are usually tried for a short time, but then abandoned, because they feel false – almost like trying to take on an acting role, trying to be someone that you are not.

So no quick fixes. Let's take the long route to enhancing and embedding your interpersonal skills – and enjoy the journey! You will find that the perspectives you gain from this exploration will take your communication skills to a whole new level.

Communication – how we think it works

We assume that we're pretty competent communicators on the whole – after all, if the conversation is important, we usually try to think about what we need to say, choose the appropriate language to use carefully, and express our ideas clearly so that the listener will understand exactly what we mean.[2] We look for indicators to confirm our success, and we will know we have achieved our objective if we receive the response we expect: a report delivered, a meeting attended, a response to an email received. We'll often look for an affective response too – indicators of rapport, shared understanding, a feeling of trust and mutual respect, a feeling of being comfortable and confident in the relationship.

While it's true to say that we're reasonably successful with routine interactions – buying a newspaper, asking for the restaurant bill, making small talk – you know from your own experience that we are not always successful. More complicated interactions have the potential to send the conversation careering off in unexpected directions!

This is mainly because the communication space is not always the quiet and orderly place we imagine it to be. Our communication can be messy, ambiguous and confused; misunderstandings can happen frequently. So what's really going on?

---

[2] For more information on this intuitive, common sense model of communication, look up Claude Shannon and Warren Weaver's 'Transmission Model': Claude E. Shannon and Warren Weaver, *The mathematical theory of communication*, University of Illinois Press, 1963. For something a little more sophisticated, see Michael Reddy's 'Conduit Metaphor' which tries to take into account various sources of noise that muddy our communications: Michael Reddy, 'The conduit metaphor: a case of frame conflict in our language about language', in A. Ortony (ed.), *Metaphor and thought* (pp. 284–310), Cambridge University Press, 1979. For even more detail, see Dean Barnlund's 'Transactional model of communication', in C. D. Mortensen (ed.), *Communication theory*, 2nd edition (pp. 47–57), Transaction, 2008.

Communication – how it really works

When we are talking with others we tend to assume that we are at the centre of what is happening and firmly in control of what is happening! In reality communication is usually more complex. Communication 'messages' pass rapidly back and forth between us in a continuous flow, as we turn our thoughts into communication messages, and communication messages we receive into thoughts.

Verbal and non-verbal communication is more than just an ebb and flow of listening and speaking; it is really a continuous exchange and adjustment of communication, with the communicators sending and receiving messages simultaneously in a dynamic, interdependent, multi-layered and continuous feedback system. Indeed there are so many messages being sent at any one time that many of them may not even be received, at least not consciously, while other messages are sent unintentionally!

All the while we are busily engaged in interpreting and responding to information as we receive it, picking up on verbal and non-verbal communication cues, evaluating and re-evaluating our understanding – trying to figure out what the cues mean within the context of the conversation, our own expectations, assumptions, perspectives and norms of behaviour, personality types and preferences, past experiences, and so on – and adjusting our responses accordingly.

The ambiguity and uncertainty of this shifting environment has the potential to create 'noise' or interference in the communication, so sometimes our interpretations are correct – at other times not. If we notice some kind of communications breakdown (perhaps a pause in the interaction or the puzzled expression of the other person), we'll check – ask questions, repeat back, rephrase or summarise what we think we've heard. Sometimes we are

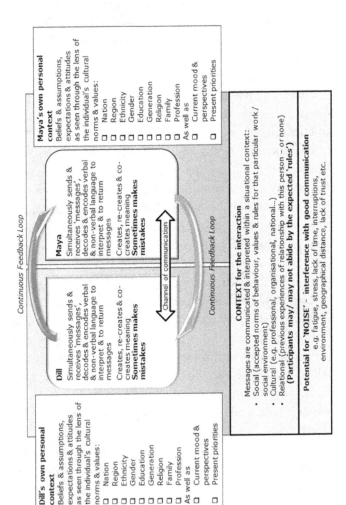

How communication works

oblivious to the fact that we've got it wrong – or at least, that we haven't understood the full message that the other person meant to convey. In such instances we may only realise that there was a communication gap some time later when reflecting back on the conversation.

In such a complex environment, understanding cannot always be assumed. Even ordinary words – *professional, efficient, delegate, empower* – can be subject to wide variations of interpretation as individuals make decisions about what the word means to them, and what its connotations may be in a particular context. Being aware of how word meanings may be interpreted differently makes participants more alert to the possibilities of misinterpretation, and therefore more intentional about communicating with clarity.

Even when we are speaking the same language there's often a difference between what we say and what we mean; our capacity to bridge this gap is what makes us truly brilliant as communicators. In order to manage the complex communication process, we humans tend to become quite adept at shifting position within the interaction in order to gain more information and so get closer to understanding what might be the stated – as well as the hidden – meaning.

The importance of context

The effectiveness of communication relies heavily on the degree to which the communicators share (and therefore understand) the context(s) in which they are communicating:

> ➢ social context: stated or unstated norms of behaviour, social conventions, values, rules and laws

> ➢ cultural context: lifestyle and identity – nationality, race, gender, sexual orientation, ethnicity, class, caste – which will influence attitudes, beliefs, mind-sets

> ➤ relational context: type of relationship, previous interpersonal history, pre-established norms, expected behaviours

In order to be effective, both the sender and receiver must have access to a sort of 'code book' of shared understanding. Let's take the example of a simple question: 'Have you eaten yet?' Depending on who the participants are in this interaction, the interpretation and understanding of what is meant by this question will vary. What do *you* think this means? Here are some options:

> ➤ A mother talking to her child – showing maternal concern?

Have you eaten yet?

> ➤ An indirect invitation for a lunch or dinner date?

> ➤ A polite greeting common around mealtimes in China?

You will respond appropriately if you know the context and therefore what is expected and 'normal' in that situation. However, this shared knowledge cannot always be assumed, so part of the responsibility of the expert communicator is to lay the foundations for a shared 'code book'. In teams this starts with talking about how you want to work together – identifying your shared purpose, your values, your priorities and thinking about the qualities and skills each member of the team brings to the joint endeavour. This kind of 'contracting' conversation needs to be refreshed regularly as the team matures together, as new colleagues join the team, and as the team faces new challenges or organisational change. Opening up the communication in this way will raise your skills as communicators to a whole new level and lay the foundations for solid working relationships.

In teams this shared 'code book' will also contain a range of communication short-cuts – technical words, jargon, acronyms and other abbreviations which are specific to your professional field. Using these 'short-cuts' is very efficient – but of course can be bewildering to newcomers, or clients and customers not in your field. In this case you and your colleagues become translators and interpreters!

If you share the same context, experiences and assumptions, communication is much more likely to be successful. However, these shared sources of information, as well as enabling understanding, also have the potential to derail the communication process. While shared context allows us to take communication short-cuts (partners, families, old friends and people who have worked together for a long time are particularly good at this), leaning too heavily on shared assumptions can also pose problems if those assumptions are never discussed openly: teams can fall into lazy habits; new colleagues can feel excluded; friends – and even partners – can drift apart; communication channels can dry up through lack of use.

At such times you'll need to be more intentional about checking that everyone involved still shares the same understanding; get to know each other again, talk through potential similarities and differences, and establish common ground. Within your team, have a new contracting conversation to remind yourselves of your shared purpose and values.

Managing communications 'noise'

Troublesome interference can impede the communication process between participants at any time, even when there's a shared context. Even if the speaker tries to communicate a clear and accurate message, it may not be accurately received and interpreted. Identifying sources of 'noise', or interference – and where possible managing them – can greatly enhance your communication and the communication within the team.

Of course, some interference may be *actual* noise in the environment – the noise of phones ringing, fingers tapping on keyboards, building work going on outside, the hubbub of conversations – all of which distracts our attention, making it harder for us to think and speak clearly, and listen accurately.

Other kinds of interference come from language – for example, we don't choose the most appropriate wording, or we deliver the right words with the wrong tone or intonation. The noise may also come from the communicators themselves!

Here are some more examples:

Sources of noise which can interfere with good communication		
Language-based noise	*Noise from within – the speaker or listener*	*Environmental noise*
Different understandings about word meanings Accent/ intonation Jargon/technical language or abbreviations not shared Message unclear/ ambiguous	Fatigue/stress Individual perceptions, attitudes, opinions, emotions Attitude towards the speaker or the message Different priorities Lack of trust, defensiveness	Inappropriate place/context for the conversation Work environment, poor workspace design Technological problems with communication networks, IT systems

Mismatch verbal/ non-verbal signals creates dissonance – makes interpreting the message more difficult	Filtering – past experiences influencing current interpretation	Geographical distance Information overflow and lack of time

Do any of these sound familiar to you? Communication 'noise' can never be eliminated, but simply by being aware of what's going on and thinking about how you (and the team) might address the issue, it is possible to reduce the potential for this kind of interference to undermine effective communication. (This is clearly easier with some types of communications noise than others.)

Communicating with oneself, to better communicate with others

Growing up as the eldest child in a family of ten, Kerry quickly assumed the role of unofficial mum, taking care of her siblings and keeping order in the household. This early experience made her an assertive communicator and an efficient organiser. In her professional life her readiness to take on responsibilities and follow-through on projects earned her considerable respect and quick promotion. However relationships with her team were often strained: while recognising her strengths, team members could feel intimidated by her degree of assertiveness and tendency to tell rather than ask. Colleagues began to feel frustrated and disempowered – their combined expertise and experience seemed to be of no value, so they disengaged. Kerry became increasingly isolated from her team and overloaded with work; eventually she had to take six months' leave due to stress.

We've talked about how our communication with others is powerfully influenced by factors acting within: our personality traits and preferences; our upbringing, which influences our attitudes and values; the foundations on which we have built our professional life, including education and training; our past life experiences, and more recent influences; our current role; the culture of the organisation where we work. Any of these could be having a dominant or lingering effect on our thinking and behaviour, which might be positive, or less so.

You don't need years of counselling to understand what might be going on for you in the background when you are communicating with others. You simply need to know yourself (although that's sometimes a tough challenge isn't it?). For example, if you have a tendency to perfectionism, or a chronic lack of confidence, or a strong moral compass, these will often have their roots in deeply established patterns of thinking or living instilled by others and then incorporated into your behaviour and ways of being. Being curious about the impact these factors might be having on your interpersonal communication is an indication that you're on your way to becoming a skilled and effective communicator.

Lastly there are the additional random external factors that can interfere with our communication with others – the stuff that happens to be going on in our lives at the time and which forms a kind of backcloth to the interaction. Even while we are engaged in the conversation and apparently focused on the matter in hand, our thoughts and preoccupations may be distracting our attention. At such times we will need to make a bigger effort to concentrate.

The communication space can be a crowded place – sometimes we need to be intentional about de-cluttering so that we can make room for connecting with others.

Non-verbal communication cues

Part of the complexity of our interactions is the range of non-verbal cues that we assimilate, often unconsciously, when interacting with others. The subject of non-verbal communication is an entirely separate and complex field, but briefly, we read non-verbal communication cues from multiple sources to help us work out the meaning of what is being communicated. Most of the time we expect a congruence between the words and the non-verbal cues. For example, during a presentation the intonation and tone, together with the animated expression of the speaker, would lead the listener to conclude that he/she is passionate about the subject.

When the non-verbal cues don't match the words being uttered, we are left wondering what is really going on. Imagine an apparently empathic statement to a colleague who has been made redundant, or whose relationship is breaking up, being delivered with a bright and cheery tone while the speaker is checking their mobile or looking out of the window.

The mismatch between the words and the speaker's tone of voice, the lack of eye contact, and their lack of attention as they attempt to multi-task on their mobile may well lead the listener to conclude that the speaker is being insincere, indifferent to his/her situation or even ironical.

In situations where we become aware of a mismatch (dissonance) between the words and the non-verbal signals, we tend to place more weight on messages we receive through the non-verbal signals we observe, rather than the words we hear.[3]

Here is a brief overview of non-verbal communication cues:

use of space (proxemics): the personal space 'bubble', or invisible boundary within which individuals feel comfortable when with others

body language (kinesics): posture, gesturing, body movement, facial expression, eye contact

sounds (paralanguage): tone, pitch, intonation, pauses and silence

use of time (chronemics): the way in which individuals allocate their time – indicator of rapport, respect and status

physical contact (haptics): touch, including shaking hands, holding, embracing, pushing, or patting on the back

objects (artefacts): the environment, the objects in that environment, and the way in which they are arranged

---

[3] The 7%-38%-55% Rule proposed by Albert Mehrabian is often misrepresented in this context. His research, begun in the 1960s, was based on a specific and limited sample and was not intended to refer to communication in general. Clearly communication messages require more than 7% words for the communication to be successful. What we can say is that non-verbal communication can sometimes have greater impact than words when it comes to detecting attitudes and emotions, and that the extent to which we rely on non-verbal cues to make meaning will vary from one situation to another.

Interpreting 'clusters' of non-verbal cues

We are constantly reading complex non-verbal cues to gain information about relationships. We use our observations to interpret the level of engagement in the interaction; the degree of rapport and trust; differences of status; mental states – feelings, emotions; agreement or disagreement, and so on. However, it's important to note that non-verbal communication signals do not usually function independently or even sequentially but rather as clusters of behaviour, for example:

> ➢ Looking out of the window could be an indication that the person is reflecting on a problem...

However:

> ➢ Window gazing, combined with yawning, sighing, and eye-rolling, may well suggest boredom, disengagement and irritation

Non-verbal communication is also extremely economical and efficient, making it possible to transmit several messages at once. For example, during an interaction with their team, a manager may be smiling to show friendliness, keeping eye contact to show assertiveness and nodding to show agreement, all at the same time.

Often we convey these messages unconsciously – our thoughts seeping through the very pores of our skin through 'micro-messages' (more about this in Chapter 15). It can be useful to get feedback from others as to how they are interpreting your non-verbal behaviours; you may be surprised by the accuracy of their observations! We also need to be alert; we don't always pick up on non-verbal cues, which means that we miss valuable information. As with verbal communication, we are also capable of misinterpreting non-verbal cues because of our own perspectives, assumptions or because we don't understand the context.

Although non-verbal signals for emotions tend to be shared across cultures (the work of Paul Ekman[4] suggests that there are six universal facial expressions – disgust, sadness, anger, fear, surprise, love), a huge range of non-verbal communication is, like all communication, framed within a cultural context. In British English for example, when a speaker wishes to express irony, the tone of voice will show that the words mean the opposite of the stated or ostensible one and the facial expression will remain neutral:

> Manager: 'I'm afraid I need you to work this weekend.'

> Employee (resigned and in a flat tone of voice): 'I can't think of anything I'd rather do.'

Of course, cultural context is not limited to national or regional differences – organisational, professional, social, family cultures all have their own particular cultural contexts.

Inappropriate use and misinterpretations of non-verbal communication can build barriers rather than enhance understanding, can create mistrust, or even be interpreted as insensitive, impolite, rude or aggressive. Communications are often messed up due to 'user error'.

---

[4] Paul Ekman, *Non-verbal messages: cracking the code: my life's pursuit*, Paul Ekman Group, 2016.

Tapping into communication 'rules'

After all we've said about the complexity of interpersonal communication, you may be thinking it's really a wonder we manage to communicate at all!

Although there are many sources of potential interference in interpersonal communications, most of our communication is reasonably successful because we can tap into a repertoire of shared communicative or sociolinguistic 'rules' – the ultimate 'shared code book'. These rules govern the way in which participants are expected to behave during a conversation:

> ➢ the importance of taking turns in a conversation and how 'airtime' is shared between participants

> ➢ the acceptability (or otherwise) of interrupting or 'over-talking'

> ➢ the importance of 'small talk' ('phatic' communication) in establishing and maintaining rapport

> ➢ what is meant by 'politeness'

We tacitly or overtly agree with other members of our community what is normal and acceptable for greetings, congratulations, apologies, thanks, etc. in order to sound genuine and appropriate rather than overly effusive, pretentious, fake, or even ridiculous.

Let's take an example of how this works by thinking about what people mean by being 'polite'. Try arranging these requests in order of politeness from most polite to least polite (I suggest you say them out loud – you'll see it makes a difference depending on whether your tone of voice is neutral, authoritative, pleading, exasperated, etc.):

> A. Jay, help here.
> B. Jay, can't you see I need help?
> C. Jay, I need help with these folders.
> D. Jay, could you please help with me with this?

You'll notice that the usual rules of politeness depend on the context of the conversation. National cultures have different codes of politeness; work cultures too. A noisy factory environment or busy emergency medical department will generally mean that shorter interactions are desirable. The acceptable level of directness and brevity also depends on the relationship between the people involved; is this a customer or client with a manager, colleagues who have just met, team members or friends who know each other well? The way in which the request is made – voice intonation, facial expression, etc. – will also convey meaning; Jay may be happy to forgo some of the politeness he would normally expect because of the context, or he may understand the other person is being polite because he/she is smiling, even if the conventional politeness formulae – *could you... please* – are absent.

Of course some people flout sociolinguistic rules – and get away with it! They may be doing so for comic effect, because they lack insight, or because they are simply unaware of the 'rules'. Often this flouting of the rules is overlooked if somehow the message gets through in the way it was intended – supported by the context, the relationship, non-verbal cues, etc. However, lack of awareness about these shared rules can also lead to communications failures ranging from minor misunderstandings and awkwardness through to a loss of trust and even conflict.

Conclusion

Communication is a complex, technical and highly personal activity, but knowing more about the technical aspects of the communication process enhances your ability to use communication tools and strategies more effectively.

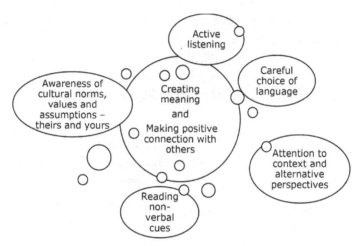

How we make connections with others through our communication

While language is of course a very important element in the communication process, we have seen that being an effective communicator is not just about finding the right words. Before we can be clear in our communication with others, we need to be clear where we're coming from when we communicate. Our values, personality preferences, attitudes, assumptions, hot buttons, motivators, drivers and personal priorities create a default mechanism for interpreting and responding to others. Unacknowledged, these influences can become unhelpful 'noise' leading to assumptions and judgements which get in the way of effective communication. When acknowledged, these personal insights enable us to communicate with empathy and compassion.

We human beings have an extraordinary capacity for communicating *brilliantly*! We just need to check that we are communicating what we *think* we are communicating, and develop an awareness of how we support or sabotage our best intentions. At its very best our communication is about more than exchanging information effectively; it is the means by which we build the kind of solid connections within our communities that enable everyone to live, work and thrive, together.

Applying this to your workplace

a) Use the communication diagram to analyse a recent interaction; try drawing your own diagram to help you to think about how the various components – participants, message, channel, feedback, context – came together

b) Look at the table showing the different sources of communications 'noise'

  ➤ Which might be relevant to your own communication and communication within the team? What steps can you take to deal with these sources of interference?

  ➤ Are there other sources of 'noise' which might apply in your particular area of work? How might you deal with these? How would this enhance your work-life and improve the performance of the team?

c) Become a people-watcher. What do you notice about the non-verbal communication of people you observe, for example, what does their posture tell you – about their assertiveness, confidence, energy levels, engagement, and so on?

Further references

➤ Apps, Judy, *The art of communication: how to be authentic, lead others and create strong connections*, Capstone, 2019

➤ Brown, Brené, *Rising strong*, Vermilion, 2015

➤ Matsumoto, David and Frank, Mark G., *Nonverbal communication: science and applications*, Sage, 2012

➤ Maxwell, John C., *Everyone communicates, few connect*, Thomas Nelson, 2010

➤ Patterson, K., Grenny, J. and Switzler, A., *Crucial conversations: tools for talking when the stakes are high*, McGraw-Hill, 2002

6

Listening heart and soul

Introduction

How good a listener would you say you are? We often think of communication as being mainly about speaking – putting yourself out there, getting your ideas across – but our capacity to listen has a major impact on the quality of our relationships with others as well as on job effectiveness. Our capacity to listen can also help to establish a feeling of rapport with others and create a sense of belonging among team members.

In this chapter we'll be thinking about what we mean by 'good listening'. We will show how you can raise your communication to a whole new level to build strong working relationships and enhance the work of the team.

Making time for listening

> You can't understand someone until you've walked a mile in their shoes.
>
> (Old American saying)

As a crucial component of relationships and communication, listening must be a top priority – which means finding time to make the mental space for conversations and whatever new insights, perspectives, information and creative solutions they may bring.

You're probably thinking that time is the one thing you don't have at work. On the other hand, if you're caught up in constant activity, how will you ever find the time to listen to your colleagues properly? Good listening doesn't lend itself to multi-tasking – and by not making the time to listen you risk ending up only listening to your own voice, which is not always the best strategy for success.

Making time for listening doesn't have to mean putting aside hours for long conversations. Being fully present with the other person to listen in a five-minute conversation can be more meaningful, and have greater impact, than two hours of exchanging 'monologues in the presence of a witness'.[1] All it requires is that you 'clear the space'; set aside what you are doing and your preoccupations at the time, clear your paperwork away, mentally disconnect from your mobile, tablet or laptop screen, shut yourself off from the surrounding noises and give the person who is speaking your total and undivided attention.

When you are listening with full attention you are showing interest and demonstrating in a very real way that the other person is being recognised and heard. Without saying a single word, attentive listening shows the other person that you think they are important and that you value them as another human being. This is the point where listening helps relationship building, even though you may disagree with what they are saying.

---

[1] Margaret Millar, 'The Weak-Eyed Bat', in *Collected Millar*, Soho Syndicate, 2017.

What gets in the way of good listening?

Good communication is a delicate balance between talking and listening. An old saying is a useful guide: *'We have two ears and only one mouth, so we should listen twice as much as we speak. Also, the ears are designed to stay open and the mouth is designed to shut.'*

Different cultures have different 'politeness rules' about the amount of time one should give to listening versus talking during a typical conversation, although we sometimes flout these conventions or get irritated when others do. From time to time we can get tired of making the effort to listen and we try to impose our own views; we give ourselves plenty of airtime, but then shut down when it comes to being on the 'receiver' end.

On other occasions we may become exhausted by the very fact of feeling that we are not being heard. Having attempted in vain to get our needs recognised, our views understood – and been ignored – we simply give up. We give up on the talking, and give up on the listening, shutting ourselves off from the engagement with the other person. Communication and the relationship break down. As Ralph Waldo Emerson said, *'There's a difference between listening and waiting your turn to talk.'* The internal conversations that take place in our heads can be every bit as loud and persistent as the words spoken aloud. Assumptions and pre-conceived ideas can create interference or 'noise' which can prevent you from hearing what the other person is really saying.

> The greatest barrier to effective communication is the tendency to evaluate what the other person is saying and therefore to misunderstand or not really to hear.
>
> (Carl R. Rogers)[2]

---

[2] Carl Rogers, *On Becoming a Person*, new edition, Robinson, 2004.

Classic examples of poor attentive listening

Have you ever been caught up in a conversation with a non-listener? In the following interactions, you will notice that what starts out as an opportunity for listening is quickly derailed by the personal agenda of the listener.

The hijacker

Alireza: Last weekend we had a great time up in the mountains. We...

Carlos: Oh I can tell you about mountains!! We spent three weeks skiing in Canada. That's the country you need to visit. You can organise the whole trip yourself if you.... Blah, blah, blah, etc. etc.

How do you feel when your story is hijacked?

The injured party, when you were looking for a bit of sympathy

Charlotte: Actually, I'm in a lot of pain. I think I broke my finger when I tripped going up the stairs. I think I...

Jenny: I know exactly how you feel. Two years ago I broke my arm in four places. I was in plaster for six months. The arm is still not right and I have to do three exercises four times a day. The first exercise is...

How can Jenny really know exactly how Charlotte is feeling?

The fixer

Craig: Fancy meeting you here in the sports centre. I have come to register for an aerobics class.

George: I strongly recommend yoga instead. You don't want to be mixing up with a load of sweaty women. I go to the 'Yoga for Guys' class on Monday evenings. The teacher is great. I've got his phone number on me. Let's phone him straight away and book you onto his class.

Note that the interjections from George, although they may have been well-intentioned, are really all about him rather than Craig.

Often you can fall short of giving the other person your full and undivided attention if you are:

➤ totally absorbed in what you are doing. You might not even turn around to face the person who is talking to you. You may give the impression that you are listening by the occasional 'oh yes, uh-huh, I see, mmm'

➤ listening selectively to what is being said, only paying attention to specific bits of information that are likely to be useful to you or may provide you with an opportunity to interrupt

Pause for reflection

In the last few days when have you been engaged in token or pretend listening, what impact is this likely to have had on your colleagues and on your working relationships?

How to do excellent attentive listening

Fully engaged, 'active' listening is hard work for beginners. It requires first a strong desire to hear what the other person is saying. This requires you to be genuinely interested in other people; not for what you can get out of them but valuing them as fellow human beings. It also requires great concentration and patience and, in certain situations, empathy. To demonstrate to your colleagues that you value them you need to listen to them attentively, only asking questions to truly understand their point of view.

There will be occasions when a colleague is expressing a high degree of emotion, even anger. When that happens, try to listen to them empathically. This means stepping into their shoes and feeling the situation as they are feeling it. You do not need to agree with what they are saying. (We'll be coming back to empathic listening later in this chapter.)

Be aware of where your attention lies – be totally present and still your mind. This is probably the greatest gift you can give your colleague. You will notice the positive effect your attention has on people and your relationship with them. Identify your own emotions about the situation and consciously put them on the back burner so that they don't interfere with your listening.

Prepare yourself for listening:

> ➤ Sit or stand in relation to the other person in such a way as to convey a sense of being comfortable, and at ease, while at the same time being attentive

> ➤ Silently breathe out and let go of any tension you may have so that you can focus on what's important to the speaker and their needs, over and above your own. Trust that you will get the opportunity

to express your views at some point... just not right now

➤ Convey a relaxed feeling of calm through body language, gesture, and an open listening posture

Get to know your own best state for listening so that you can get into that state whenever you wish. What are you like when you're listening at your best? Maybe draw a symbol that represents this state, or write it down, or just know what you're like when you're in your optimum listening mode.

Listen to yourself

Listening to yourself is not a self-indulgent, appeasing and self-justifying thing to do, but is a crucial part of the process of reflection. Listening to your inner self means taking the opportunity to acknowledge what you are feeling, realise your needs, and allow yourself to 'be' as well as 'do'. Listening to yourself also means challenging your assumptions and biases, looking out for inconsistencies between your stated values and the way you actually behave.

Listening with curiosity

When someone comes to you with a query or complaint, they may tell you directly what they're concerned about. More often they will ask you a question or make a comment at a more general level, to gauge your response before they come to what is really worrying them. You can help them to tell you their real concern, and therefore increase your chances of getting a good solution, by asking them powerful and supportive questions to get to the core of the matter. The following questions are some of your most useful allies in good listening, and you may know others which work well for you:

> ➤ Can you tell me about that?

> ➤ In what ways is that important to you?

> ➤ What's the question behind your question?

> ➤ What are you really concerned about here/deep down?

A caution about 'back-channelling'

During any conversation it's usual to give indicators that you are interested in what the person is saying, and that you are paying attention. Responding by what's called 'back-channelling' encourages the other person to keep talking and may include expressions such as *yes, indeed, go on, oh dear, really? etc.* and even short sounds such as *mmm, ah, uh-huh, oh,* etc.

However, it is perfectly possible to be on automatic pilot, punctuating what the other person is saying with the occasional *'OK', 'really?' 'is that right?'* or *'uh-huh'* without paying attention at all. If you have been on the receiving end of this yourself, you will know that this insincere token or pretend listening doesn't fool anyone – feigned attentiveness is easy to detect and can be hugely disrespectful to the other person.

Give cues that are genuinely encouraging, even when you may disagree; demonstrate that you are listening by acknowledging their point and echoing, paraphrasing, or mirroring to check understanding.

Summarising and playing back

To make sure that your own perspectives and assumptions are not distorting your understanding of what the other person is saying, reflect on what is being said and clarify your understanding by echoing or summarising or paraphrasing, and by mirroring the emotion you're hearing or seeing.

> *Echoing the exact words you have heard* helps you to check that you have heard correctly – and provides an opportunity for the other person to revisit, and possibly revise, what they have said

> *Paraphrasing* – summarise what has been said but use different words, making sure that you retain the original meaning as much as you can and that you are not adding your own interpretation. Remember to keep it tentative, so that the other person can correct you if necessary – opening responses like 'It sounds like…' or 'It seems that…' can be useful here. Paraphrasing in this way enables you to communicate that you are listening carefully, but be careful not to take over the conversation at this point. When you are sure you have understood correctly, invite the other person to continue talking

Attention generated by genuine interest, and without interruption, is important for getting excellent results. *Attentive* listening means clearing your mental clutter and putting your attention on what the other person is actually saying, being naturally curious and genuinely interested.

Asking questions

Asking questions at appropriate times during the conversation can also help the listening process. However, this isn't about constantly interrupting, jumping ahead to second guess what the person will say next, interrogating the other person, or attempting to hijack the conversation in order to steer it towards your own objectives.

Think about your reasons for asking the question:

> *to clarify*: clarifying questions to check that you have understood – 'So is it your view that…'

> *to elicit examples*: questions to invite examples which can move on the discussion – 'I'm not sure I understand what you mean – could you give me an example?'

> *to get more information*: open questions to ask for more information – 'What is the most challenging part of this for you?' – although avoid the danger of collecting information solely to satisfy your curiosity

> *to explain*: questions to explain why you need to know – 'I'm asking because…'

Use the following types of questions with care as otherwise you might derail the conversation:

> Closed questions can be limiting as they usually require only yes/no or very short answers: '*Can you use Excel?*' '*Have you emailed the report?*' Use them sparingly, for example: when you need to confirm what you think you know, obtain information, establish a pattern or sequence of events, or when offering a summary of what has been agreed before moving on in the conversation

> Question tags at the end of statements: 'You've worked with Meena before, haven't you?' But they can also be used effectively when listening empathically: 'I imagine that this has been a tough time for you and the team?'

> Leading statements can also show empathy: 'I guess you're feeling exhausted after the Frankfurt conference!' 'I imagine that was a disappointing

outcome for you after all your hard work.' They can also be helpful if you want to focus on a specific point or detail. However, use leading questions carefully as you might be pre-empting the person's real thoughts – and getting it wrong! 'Maybe you'll feel better when you've spoken to X, won't you?'

➢ Asking questions that begin with the word 'why', as the other person is likely to feel that you are being judgemental or critical e.g. 'Why did you do it that way?'

At all times remember to keep the questions short so that you don't take over the conversation.

Listening with your body

What you take in

We don't just listen with our head/brain; we take in signals from our emotions and bodily sensations.[3] Remember Mehrabian's formula for interpreting emotions and attitudes where only 7% represents the exact words, a further 38% represents the tone, pitch and energy in the voice and the remaining 55% the non-verbal communication e.g. body language. This suggests that when we listen our eyes are as important as our ears; picking up on non-verbal *as well as* verbal cues helps us understand the real meaning of what we are hearing:

➢ voice tone and intonation, pace, volume, hesitation

➢ facial expression including eye contact or loss of eye contact, frowning, smiling, raised eyebrows, yawning

---

[3] Albert Mehrabian, *Nonverbal communication*, Aldine Transaction, 2007.

> ➤ body language including posture, shifting of position, deep or shallow breathing, changes in facial colouration, movements of the small muscles either side of the mouth, gestures, e.g. hand movements, touch

> ➤ personal space 'bubble' or distance between the individuals

As we mentioned in Chapter 5, some non-verbal signals will vary according to the cultural background so remember to bear in mind the context of your communication. Keep looking out for signs of any mismatch between what is being said and the signals you are receiving and check that you have read the signals correctly using your active listening skills.

What you give out

The non-verbal signals you convey in response to this input are crucial. As you listen, make sure:

> ➤ you use supportive and encouraging gestures – nodding, smiling and eye contact

> ➤ you 'soft focus' your eyes to take in the whole person, rather than constantly looking intensely into their eyes (or over their shoulder!). Be aware of cultural differences concerning eye contact

> ➤ your tone, intonation, speed of delivery, volume, and appropriate use of pausing and silence value the other person and give them space to say what they need to say

If the person you're listening to looks away it may just indicate they are thinking. Wait and be there when they look back at you, i.e. don't follow their gaze and look where they are looking or start reading notes, or checking your mobile!

Allowing space for a comfortable silence

Sometimes the other person needs time and personal space to think through how to respond in a conversation. Perhaps they never thought about this topic before, or they are stressed or tired, or maybe you've presented them with a very complex issue for which they need time to sort out their thoughts. In order to give the other person the time they need, think about how you can create a comfortable space for the other person to clarify their thinking, and create their own light-bulb moments. If your colleague goes silent and maybe looks away, resist the temptation to fill the gap by interrupting. Hold the space and take the silence as an indicator that quality thinking may be happening. When people know that they're going to be listened to without judgement or criticism, the quality of their thinking is much richer.

Is it more than a coincidence that the words 'listen' and 'silent' are made up of the same letters?

Empathic listening

So much more than 'taking an interest' or 'being kind', empathic listening means communicating your connection with the other person.

Listening with empathy doesn't mean you have to agree with the other person. However, it does mean being in touch with that person's feelings and being aware of how those feelings might differ from your own. If a colleague says something that surprises or shocks you, give them the space to talk about how they are feeling or seeing the situation.

ear / you / eyes / undivided attention / heart

The Chinese characters that make up the verb 'to listen' tell us something significant about this skill

If the topic is sensitive, watch out for signals that the person is struggling and allow pauses for them to gather their thoughts and feelings, and simply be fully present for that person.

You may actually identify with what they are going through because you've experienced it yourself. If so, use your EQ to manage your emotions so that you don't shift the focus of the conversation to your own story – 'I know just how you're feeling – I've been there' – rather than focusing on the other person. Resist the urge to provide quick solutions, cheer them up, tell them that they are wrong, or try to reason them round to your way of thinking. Your colleague may not find it helpful if you seek to change the reality of their perspective with exhortations to 'Look on the bright side...' or 'It could be worse'. Genuine empathy means experiencing life as the other person experiences it, fully entering their world.

I'm not here to fix you. I'm not here to feel it for you. I'm here to feel it as you are feeling it and let you know that you are not alone.

(Author unknown)

At its very best you forge a relationship with a colleague in such a deep way that you help them experience hearing themselves, letting go of your own preoccupations in order to be fully present with the other. This can be mentally and emotionally exhausting, so make sure you keep breathing deeply, keep your body posture open and respond in ways that encourage them to keep talking. Often the less you say, the better. Just be there in support of the other person.

Empathic listening helps to build the trust and respect essential to a real connection. It reduces tension, allows your colleague to express feelings and emotions, allows space for even strong differences to be heard, and it creates a safe environment that is conducive to open communication and collaborative working.

Although empathic listening is not always easy, and requires effort, the rewards are well worth the effort in terms of building trust and respect. This opening up to the other person creates a safe space where they can express their ideas, thoughts, concerns, expectations and emotions; this kind of listening reduces tensions, builds relationships and encourages collaborative problem-solving.

The greatest need of the human soul is to be understood.

(Gandhi)

To summarise

Here are some tips for making the most of your listening skills:

> Clear the space (a) physically: move distracting paperwork, block the phone, avoid interruptions; and (b) mentally: set aside time to be fully present

➤ Find an appropriate space to meet. For longer conversations it's worth the effort of booking a room in advance; or go for an outdoor walk together

➤ Listen with empathy and keep your focus on the other person

➤ Demonstrate your wish to connect through your non-verbal communication

➤ Use active listening techniques to check your understanding and reassure the other person that you have correctly heard what they have said

➤ Resist the urge to fill any silences. Some of you will find this easier than others!

➤ Let go of any feeling that you need to know all the answers or indeed that you do know all the answers

➤ Listen to yourself so that you are better able to listen to others

➤ Notice when you start to feel defensive or resistant. Listening is about being open, so don't let your own judgements, biases and opinions get in the way

➤ Resist the temptation to interrupt or get impatient for your chance to talk. Interrupting is a waste of time – it frustrates the speaker and limits full understanding of the message, so keep listening and allow the speaker to finish

➤ Respond appropriately – assert your opinions respectfully and own them – for example, 'It's my opinion…', 'In my experience as a …' – while also acknowledging theirs

Conclusion

Good listening is a model for respect and understanding but it takes effort, concentration and determination, so be intentional with your listening. When you are in conversation with another person give them the feeling that there is no one else in the world. Then you will be giving that person a gift they will never forget, and they will tell others what a special person you are!

Remind yourself that your goal is to truly hear what the other person is saying, so set aside all other thoughts to focus on listening, understanding and staying connected with the other person. Your careful listening will not only enable you to gain information and different perspectives and ideas, but it will also contribute to collaborative working and the kind of communication that is conducive to higher productivity and creative problem-solving.

Applying this to your workplace

a) What kind(s) of listening do you find yourself reverting to most of the time at work – pretend listening, selective listening, active listening? Now that you've had an opportunity to think again about your listening skills, what would you like to improve?

b) For an exercise on Active Listening please go to www.learningcorporation.co.uk/Library and download a copy. Think of your own examples – perhaps from recent conversations at work – and try out the echoing, summarising, paraphrasing and mirroring techniques

Further references

➢ Daniels, Robin, *Listening: hearing the heart*, Instant Apostle, 2017

➢ Hartley, Tamsin, *The listening space: a new path to personal discovery*, The Listening Space, 2017

➢ Kline, Nancy, *Time to think: listening to ignite the human mind*, Cassell, 2002

➢ Ready, Romilla and Burton, Kate, *NLP for dummies*, John Wiley & Sons, 2015

➢ If you are interested in generative (creative) thinking, you can find an introduction by going to www.learningcorporation.co.uk/Library and downloading a copy

Part two

Handling the everyday stuff

7

Things we haven't talked about: how are we going to work together and what are our values?

Introduction

In our experience we find that the culture in many organisations is focused primarily on the work that needs to be done, the outcomes to be met and the personal targets to be achieved. The answer to the question, how are we going to work together to meet these targets, is usually left to individuals to sort out for themselves.

Probably one of these, or a similar scenario, resonates with you:

> *I will be working closely with Szolt and Sophie for the foreseeable future. Is there a way in which we can contract with each other how we want to work together? If so, hopefully, this will avoid unintentional misunderstandings and a lot of wasted time.*

Although I don't have the word manager in my job title, I have been asked to lead a project that's likely to last 10–15 months. My five team members are coming from all parts of the organisation. I would like to involve them fully from the outset. What type of plan could we put together?

Janet, who is a very hard worker, has caused havoc in our department by losing her temper again. No one wants to work with her. Why don't we have some sort of departmental 'code of 'behaviour'?

In this chapter we continue to focus on the practicalities of working well together. Even if you do not have a management or a supervisory role, we assume that you are the sort of person who steps up to the plate when you see areas where performance could be improved. First, we introduce two tools that have proved beneficial to people working in teams, on projects or in other types of working groups. Then we cover the importance of having an agreed code of shared values and behaviours.

Holding the Mirror

This tool, which we call 'Holding the Mirror', can be useful in the following types of situations:

> ➤ You have been asked to head up or become a member of a small team where you will be working together for at least six months; or

> ➤ You have been working together in a small team for several months. Whilst things have been reasonably OK there have been some bumps and hiccups in relationships which you all want to avoid in future; or

> ➤ There has been ongoing, serious disruption in your group and the people involved have either

proactively decided to call a truce and agree how to work well together in future, or, more likely, they have been told to stop their disruptive behaviour and sort things out, perhaps with the support of HR or a coach

The Holding the Mirror process operates as follows. Each team member agrees to complete the form and then holds 1 to 1 meetings with the other team members to share how they prefer to work, and then they contract how they will work together in future. In the case of the third situation above, after the 1 to 1 meetings have taken place, we recommend that all the team members should meet and commit to how they will interact in future.

In the final section of this chapter we explain how you can obtain a copy of this tool.

Project/team plan

It is amazing what you can accomplish if you do not care who gets the credit.

(Harry S. Truman)

A project/team plan is valuable at the formation stage of any team. We have used this tool successfully with several different types of teams and in different parts of the world.

For example, you would find this document useful if you are asked to step forward and manage a project team or help create or revitalise a Community of Best Practice. (This is a network of people in an organisation who share the same specialist technical knowledge and skill and want to set up a more structured way of exchanging knowledge, insights and best practice.)

A copy of the project/team plan is reproduced on the next page.

Project/Team Plan		
Name of team		
1.a Purpose of team	1.b Team's scope	1.c Members and connections
2.a Required outcomes	3.a Potential barriers to success	4.a Resources we need
2.b Measures of success	3.b How we will overcome barriers	4.b Comms and other systems

We recommend all the members of the team work together to create it. This activity helps to build relationships and the cohesiveness of the team. The team members would agree the following:

> ➤ The team's Purpose, the 'why' the team or Community of Best Practice exists; the Scope of the team's activities; the Membership of the team and how they are connected with relevant people in other parts of the business and with external specialists: the 'who'

> ➤ The Required Outcomes and their related Measures of Success. This is the 'what' that needs to be done by certain deadlines. By 'measures of success' we mean the evidence needed to demonstrate that each of the outcomes has been met

> ➤ A further essential step is to discuss and agree the Potential Barriers the team is likely to face and the proactive steps they will take to Overcome the Barriers. Without this tool these two critically important steps are likely to be overlooked. Typical Barriers are lack of expertise in a particular area, working in a matrix system where members could be pulled in different directions, or working virtually in different time zones

> ➤ The Resources needed, e.g. specialist equipment, a budget for time and money, expert assistance, office space and the Communication and other systems they will use

It may take two or more meetings to complete this action plan but this investment in time helps bring all the members together. It aids communication, helps all members to move forward in the same direction and it saves time in the longer run by reducing confusion.

Shared values and behaviours

> Remember the three R's: Respect for self; Respect for others; Responsibility for all your actions.
>
> (Dalai Lama)

As the name suggests, 'values' represent moral principles and generally accepted standards that are particularly important to us. They are a key ingredient of what motivates us. Examples of values are openness, respect, honesty, excellence and encouragement.

Using a metaphor from IT, values and their related behaviours are like the operating system of a team or organisation. For example, a team may have clear goals and action plans, but their achievement may be jeopardised if a virus such as dysfunctional behaviour is present in the team.

One example of dysfunctional behaviour we encountered was a manager who was exceptionally courteous when in the presence of clients or at the firm's social functions but who was like a tyrant back in the office.

Another situation we recall was to do with the value 'respect'. A manager withdrew from being involved with her colleagues and when challenged said that she was not being respected. This amazed her colleagues as she was notorious for not respecting her colleagues. This was an example of what is known as 'projection'. Projection is where an individual is blind to one of their own weaknesses but is quick to spot the same weakness in another person and is often openly critical of this other person's behaviour.

First take the plank out of your own eye, and then you will see clearly to remove the speck from your brother's eye.

(Jesus of Nazareth)

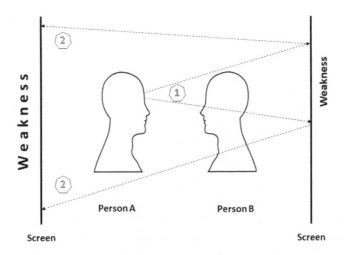

1. Person A spots a weakness in Person B. Person A is unaware, or in denial, that they also have this weakness. Person A projects their weakness onto Person B and may be openly critical of Person B. This projection is represented by dotted lines from A to B.

2. However, the dotted lines bouncing back from Person B to Person A (like the light from a cine projector reflecting from a cinema screen) indicate that Person A's weakness in that behaviour is more noticeable to other team members than Person B's behaviour.

Hopefully, your organisation already uses a short list of core values supported by examples of the sorts of behaviour that provide evidence of how each value operates in practice. If not, and you would like to be involved in creating a set of values and behaviours for your office or department, we have included a process on the website. There is a link at the end of this chapter.

Conclusion

In conclusion, working each day with shared values and behaviours increases the level of trust and helps everything run smoothly. If you are likely to be working with the same colleagues or team over many months you now have tools to not only get you started but also to help you rebuild or revitalise a relationship or a team.

If your office or department does not have a code of conduct, you could share the process in this chapter with your line manager. To help you do this there are tips on influencing in the next chapter!

Applying this to your workplace

a) What are your personal core values? Are they conducive to good working relationships?

b) What have you read that is prompting you to want to:

   ➢ improve one or more of your key relationships; or

   ➢ suggest how the relationships in one of the groups you work with could be more effective?

c) If you would like to use the Holding the Mirror exercise, you can download a copy by going to www. learningcorporation.co.uk/Library. Also on this website there is a process for creating a set of shared values and behaviours

Further references

➢ Leigh, Andrew and Maynard, Michael, *Leading your team – how to involve and inspire your team*, Nicholas Brealey, 2002

➢ Sinek, Simon, *Leaders eat last: why some teams pull together and others don't*, Penguin, 2017

➢ West, Michael, *Effective teamwork: practical lessons from organizational research*, 3rd edition (Psychology of Work and Organizations), Wiley-Blackwell, 2012

➢ Wheelan, Susan A., *Creating effective teams: a guide for members and leaders*, 5th edition, Sage Publications, 2015

8

No-con, no-sham influencing

Introduction

Most people nowadays work in fast-paced, pressured environments, where technology, downsizing and cost-cutting mean that employees need to take more responsibility, act on their own initiative and pull together to deal with increasingly complex problems.

With fewer traditional hierarchies, fewer middle managers and more inter-department working, team members frequently have less access to their managers. This is especially so if they work in a matrix, virtual or network organisation where their managers are based in other locations. When working with clients, we often hear that individuals feel they are not able to influence, with statements like:

If I was in charge, we would have direct access with our end customers and not have to rely on our distributors to tell us what our real customers want. But I don't have the authority.

I know how we could improve cross-functional working but how can I persuade my boss?

Influencing is an essential component of interpersonal skills. So, now more than ever, individuals need to be able to take greater personal responsibility and develop their own influencing skills to get things done. Is this where you are now? If so, read on...

The ethics of influencing

Many people feel reluctant to try to influence because it feels like manipulation. The key difference between manipulation and influencing with integrity is that manipulation aims for 'win-lose' – i.e. I win, you lose. Influencing with integrity aims at a win for all parties – the influence is based on a mind-set about what would be the best outcome for all involved, not just for the influencer.

Influencing with integrity can help relationships to work better and get things done more effectively. Indeed, in the twenty-first century it is no longer possible to impose your will on your colleague; you need to work with them to find the best solution and involve them in the change process.

That is what we will talk about in this chapter.

Who influenced you with integrity?

Think about those who have had the most powerful influence in your life. It may have been your parents or a specific relative, teacher, manager, or friend. What qualities did they have that you really respected?

These people probably valued you as a person, recognised your potential, your qualities as well as your skills, and encouraged you in your efforts to be the best that you could be. It's about their character; the way that they speak; the way that they listen; the way in which personal, organisational and professional values are honoured; the way they behave; the actions they take and the outcomes of those actions. As we have suggested throughout this book, honouring personal values such as honesty, integrity, compassion, respect and trust is key, without which influencing strategies amount to no more than cynical manipulation.

You will notice that certain people seem to be 'hubs' of influence. They may be more experienced, but not necessarily; they may carry some responsibility in the team, but again, not necessarily. They are the 'go-to' people we mentioned in Chapter 1 – the people who always seem to have time for *you*, even when they're busy; they genuinely care about others and their well-being; they know how to truly listen and empathise; they show awareness and perception. They can be counted on for a consistent, balanced and perceptive response; they leave you feeling better about yourself and energised to face the next challenge.

Such a relationship doesn't depend on rank or status for its effectiveness but on the environment of mutual trust and respect that people with influence create. Exercising your personal influence doesn't mean waiting until you are in a role of official responsibility – you can start thinking about your personal influence in this way at any time in your career.

Personal reflection

Look around your organisation for colleagues who influence with integrity. What specific aspect of their character or behaviour could you model yourself on?

Who you are as a person

We tend to think that influencing is all about what you do. In fact, looking at the list of qualities in the influencers described above, first and foremost it's about who you are.

Looking at it from the receiving end, I'm sure you'd agree that if you're going to permit yourself to be influenced by someone, the influencer should have most of the following qualities:

➢ likeability/friendliness

➢ trustworthiness

➢ win-win-win mind-set, i.e. a win for you, a win for me and a win for the team/organisation/client

➢ willingness to share knowledge

➢ clear sense of direction

➢ consideration towards and empowering of others

➢ confidence

➢ courage and commitment

➢ willingness to change their opinion

➢ passion for their field of work and/or personal success

Personal reflection

Which of these qualities do you know you already have? Which ones would it be good to develop a bit more in yourself?

Establishing your credibility

When you want to influence, it's much easier when you are in a position of authority – then it's simply about getting other people to come with you on the journey. What you control or influence does not need anyone else's permission.

More often than not you do not have this level of authority. You are more likely to influence successfully if you have credibility with the people you want to influence. See Chapter 2 on how to build credibility. Time spent now getting to know key people and building relationships will pay dividends in the future if you ever need to influence them. Consider what 'assets' you can offer, for example:

> ➢ How close are you to some of your major clients? Do you know their plans? What additional services would interest them? Are they using any of your products or services in a special way which might be of interest to other clients or to your product development team?

> ➢ Do you have specialist knowledge or experience or contacts that colleagues would find valuable?

> ➢ Are you friendly with any member of the executive team or do you know what is going on in other parts of the organisation?

Your credibility also depends on your reliability – if you establish a track record of delivering what you promise, living your values, then people will be more likely to listen to you when you want to influence them. If the situation doesn't allow you the time to develop that track record, who can you bring into the influencing team who does have that track record and credibility with the person you want to influence? This person may be one of those 'hubs of influence' in your team that we mentioned earlier. It is their energy and commitment to their purpose that colleagues respond to and often seek to emulate.

If you still feel nervous about influencing, how about building a coalition of like-minded colleagues and preparing a joint proposal? You might also get some comfort from Grace Hopper's quotation, *'It is better to ask for forgiveness than permission'*, and reassurance from the book *Feel the Fear and Do It Anyway* by Susan Jeffers.[1]

Your influencing mind-set

One of the key qualities listed above is a win-win-win mindset. We introduced relationship mind-sets at the end of Chapter 1 and discussed mind-sets more generally in Chapter 4. Now let's build on this by considering in more detail the win-lose and the win-win mindsets:

Self-centred mind-set (win-lose)	*Collaborative mind-set (win-win)*
The other person is my adversary	I see both of us as joint problem-solvers
The goal will be a victory for me, so I'm out to win	I'm looking for a wise decision with a win-win-win outcome
I'm only concerned about the effect on me and my job role	I will connect the topic to the other person's job role and concerns
I will try and convince the other party that my position is the only correct one, applying pressure if necessary	I want to explore the underlying interests of both sides and be open to fresh options

---

[1] Susan Jeffers, *Feel the fear and do it anyway*, Vermilion, 2007.

I will react to any concerns from the other party by arguing against them	I will treat the other person with respect and ask for any concerns in a reflective and non-reactive way
If any concessions are made it will only be from the other party	We will work together to determine who gets what
If necessary, I will take an extreme negotiating position in case I have to compromise	I will focus on shared purpose and beliefs and be reasonable throughout the meeting

Personal reflection

Where do you tend to sit in relation to these two mind-sets? If your mind-set is mainly in the left-hand column, what could be the benefits of moving more towards the right-hand column?

Influencing by listening

I will only be influenced by you if I sense you can also be influenced by me.

We tend to think that influencing is about convincing or even telling the other person what to do. If we do that, we're trying to impose our world view on them, and you can be pretty sure that they don't see the world exactly as you do and will push back (see Chapter 4).

You first need therefore to understand the planet they live on – you need to give them a good listening to. We often underestimate the sheer power of listening – and being listened to. The black musician Daryl Davis is a powerful illustration. For over 20 years, he has been befriending members of the Ku Klux Klan (the members of which advocate extremist reactionary positions such as white supremacy, white nationalism and anti-Semitism). During that time, he has – incredibly – even managed to get members to change their opinion and disavow the Klan.[2]

Daryl Davis's experience is a striking reminder that listening, and understanding, is an essential first step to influencing. There are a lot of practical tips about listening in Chapter 6.

Influencing and change

Influencing is about generating change – you want to change the status quo in some way. People often feel threatened by change, particularly when they feel it is imposed on them. A model that can help you understand what is important to you when a major change is in the air is the SCARF model.

Drawing on extensive social neuroscience studies, David Rock[3] developed this seemingly simple framework based on studies into how and which parts of the brain react to different types of stimuli related to social interactions, such as influencing and change.

---

[2] Daryl Davis's experience is brought to life in the film *Accidental Courtesy* (2017).

[3] David Rock, *Your brain at work*, Harper Business, 2009.

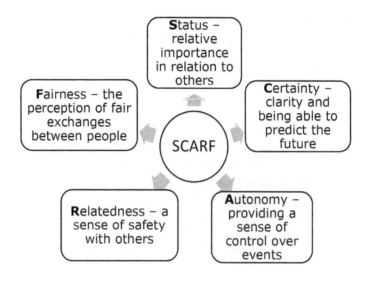

The SCARF model refers to five domains of experience

You can use this model to help you understand the range of possible reactions to the influencing you're trying to do. Let's assume you want to effect a significant change at work, and you are wondering how best to go about influencing your colleagues. Some colleagues may see your proposal as a potential threat. Others will be less concerned about themselves but worried about their team members. You will need to be sensitive to this. Here are some examples of their questions that you can anticipate:

Personal preference	Typical questions
Status	How will this affect my position in the organisation/team? Will I still be able to get out and about to meet important people?
Certainty	Will I still act for the same clients? When can I have more details about this change?

Autonomy	Currently my manager gives me a lot of freedom. Will this continue?
Relatedness	Will I still be able to sit next to Gemma and Jurgen?
Fairness	How will this affect my team leader and team members? Will anyone have to leave the team?

Incidentally, the SCARF model can be mapped onto the three main motivating drivers we mention in Chapter 9: 'S' is like Driver C, 'C' and 'A' feature strongly in Driver A, and 'R' and 'F' correspond with Driver B.

Considering people's different preferences towards change

There is a commonly held and false assumption that no one likes change, but if you think a colleague is likely to put up barriers to a change that you want to propose, be prepared in advance for what might happen. We all have different preferences about the possible introduction of a change at work. Bearing in mind that people's preferences depend on the type of change being proposed, here are some common preferences:

Instant – change it straight away	Delay
Total change	Partial, phased over time
Away from present dissatisfaction	Towards attractive vision
Reactive – take a back seat	Proactive – take a lead
Start up a project	Close things down
Need for more data	Rely on own intuition

Which of the above are your preferences? What do you know about the preferences of the person/people you're most likely to want to influence? If you don't know, how can you find out?

Preparing for a major meeting involving influencing

So far in this chapter we've been talking about how the power of positive influence comes from *you* – your friendliness, your ability to build rapport and credibility with those around you, your strengths, your values, your sense of purpose and your communication skills, including listening and your sensitivity to the needs of others. Looking around any team and seeing influencing skills in action among colleagues, it's possible to have the impression that the power of influence comes without effort – and indeed it often does happen naturally – but if you have a particular objective in mind, influencing requires thinking and planning.

There will be occasions when you want to propose a major change that will need careful planning. In these instances, make time before any such meeting to prepare a written meeting plan. At the end of this chapter you will find a link to obtain a copy of an Influence Meeting Plan.

Below are some key aspects which need to form part of your influencing preparation.

Your proposal and how you will present it

In all situations:

> ➤ Assess your level of rapport and trust, especially credibility, with the person you want to influence; what can you do to build it higher?

> ➤ Find out, perhaps from a 'go-to' person, what the other person's priorities and preoccupations might be and pitch your proposal accordingly

➤ Connect your proposal to the organisation's 'bottom line' whenever possible – for example, how it will improve profitability, cash flow, customer satisfaction, staff retention, bonuses, or efficiencies?

➤ Prepare what you want to say in a way that the other person can relate to

Put yourself in the other person's shoes

➤ Think about how you may be perceived by others. You may be passionate about what you see as the best way forward, but remember, as mentioned above, if you come across as being inflexible, others are likely to start erecting barriers and you will find it difficult to persuade and influence

➤ People often start influencing with a self-centred mind-set and when failure looms, they switch to a collaborative mind-set. That switch tends not to work because the damage has already been done and/or that person no longer comes across as being authentic

➤ It is usually difficult to make progress by using a logical approach if the other party feels highly emotional about the issue. In this situation it is preferable to listen empathically until the level of emotion eases

➤ People always do or say things for a reason that makes sense to them at the time, even if it doesn't make sense to you – so try to understand their reasons

Surface any self-limiting beliefs you may have

As part of the planning stage it is important to surface any likely self-limiting beliefs (Chapter 4), which could be for example:

> ➤ The person I want to influence is far too important to want to listen to me

> ➤ I have never tackled anything on this scale before

> ➤ I'm afraid that my proposal will be rejected, and I will look very foolish

> ➤ Their problems and priorities are different from mine

> ➤ They will think I have an ulterior motive, e.g. to take someone else's job

> ➤ The need for change is blindingly obvious. Do I need to go through all this stress?

Chapter 4 includes a process for challenging your self-limiting beliefs.

There may of course be real barriers to your ability to influence this person, and it is important to surface these too. It is helpful to spend time with a qualified coach or an experienced, trusted colleague so you can talk through any blockers and explore ways of overcoming or minimising them.

During the meeting

Throughout the meeting it will be helpful to bear the following in mind:

> ➤ The way you present your idea is as important as the content itself; keep your mind-set on win-win and stay grounded

> ➤ Meet the other person where they are, i.e. put yourself in their shoes. If the other person is angry/worried/disappointed, frustrated... then meet them where they are at that moment:

> ➤ Listen attentively to the other person. Remember that empathic listening is not a quick fix or a ruse to get people to do what you want – really listen and stay with it for the time they need

> ➤ Pace: loosely mirror their emotions as you read them – the speed at which they are talking, facial expressions, their gestures and their posture will give you clues

> ➤ Lead: stay with their emotional state until they are ready to move away from that state. Check that they are ready to move on and see if they follow you

➤ Use language intentionally – for example:

> ➤ 'It seems that' is often gentler and more effective than either 'it is' (usually just your opinion) or 'you are' (again, just your opinion)

> ➤ Change statements into questions – for example, 'How can we work together to…?' 'I wonder what it would be like if we…?'

> ➤ Capture their imagination, for example by painting a picture of the exciting future this change will help to bring about

➤ Stay with a collaborative mind-set:

> ➤ Seek the other person's ideas and build a solution together

> ➤ Think win-win-win – that is, a win for you, for the other person and for the client, organisation or team

> ➤ Avoid either/or thinking. In any situation there are always more than two options so openly explore three or more. (See implications thinking in Chapter 4)

If you get stuck

Your efforts may be met with a variety of responses – you may get:

> ➤ 'Yes' – a clear agreement and commitment to the new behaviour, attitude, or change of policy or process that you are trying to promote

> ➤ 'Yes... but/maybe' – a mixed response where the other person may seem to be agreeing but is still resisting and may be determined to seek an opportunity to revert to their original behaviour or delay in giving the go-ahead. Think what might be getting in the way here. Then ask them what further questions they have or if there is any additional information they might need

> ➤ 'No' – a clear refusal or outright resistance/ defiance. Ask them what would have made your proposal acceptable. Then consider adapting your proposal and re-presenting it

If you don't receive an instant and clear 'Yes', don't assume that a tougher approach is required or that your efforts have been in vain. Go back to 'seeking first to understand' – ask the person to tell you more about their concerns, or what would need to be in place for them to agree. Above all, accept that it will take time; influencing for change can be a slow burn.

Conclusion

> Example is not the main thing in influencing others.
> It is the only thing.
>
> (Albert Schweitzer)

When you are in a leadership or management role you can emulate good leaders by creating a shared vision, explaining why change is necessary, opening a discussion, agreeing the direction and continuing to be sensitive to your colleagues' concerns. Exercising your positive influence doesn't mean being blind to obstacles or challenges. Instead bring these out into the open and explore ways to overcome them.

Influencing for change is not a one-shot affair and may not be effective if it relies on just one person. As a stepping stone towards achieving your goal you could build a coalition with one or more colleagues who share your ideas, and create a shared view. Don't be distracted – as you see change happening, express appreciation for any efforts made by individuals and the team as a whole and remember to celebrate your joint achievements along the way together.

Applying this to your workplace

a) Having read this chapter on influencing, which skills do you already possess, and which ones do you want to develop?

b) Re-read the table on collaborative and self-centred mind-sets. Which current mind-set(s) would you like to shift to the right to become more collaborative? Conversely, are there any areas where you are too far to the right and where, because you are too considerate, you often end up with lose-win outcomes?

c) Think of two hypothetical organisational changes which could be relevant to your organisation and affect you, e.g. announcing a restructuring or a merger with another department/company. Look back at the SCARF model and the paragraph on people's different preferences towards change. Which of your basic motivators would become threatened and which of your preferences towards change would become prominent?

d) If you would like to use our pro forma Influence Meeting Plan go to www.learningcorporation.co.uk/Library and download a copy.

Further references

➤ Carnegie, Dale & Associates, *How to win friends and influence people in the digital age*, Simon & Schuster, 2012

➤ Cialdini, Robert, *Pre-suasion: a revolutionary way to influence and persuade*, Random House Business, 2017

➤ Rock, David, *Your brain at work: strategies for overcoming distraction, regaining focus, and working smarter all day long*, Harper Business, 2009

9

Getting going and keeping going: motivating myself and others

Introduction

Countless books on leadership and management have been written over the last 70 years and one might expect, by now, that our organisations would be full of highly motivated and fulfilled employees. Surveys by the CIPD[4] and other organisations indicate that there are still many organisations and individuals who struggle to keep energy levels and satisfaction alive in their work.

What gets *you* out of bed in the morning, and keeps you going, even when things at work are tough? How do you motivate yourself when the rewards are absent or when what you see or hear in your workplace is de-motivating? How individuals respond in these situations is what makes the difference – and sources of motivation are many and varied. For example, financial reward alone is not the motivator it

---

[4] CIPD/Halogen Talent Management, *Employee outlook – employee views on working life*, CIPD, 2017.

is often assumed to be.[5] The truth is that what motivates you is likely to be different from what motivates other people, which is why getting buy-in when colleagues are tired, under pressure or even not as engaged or enthused by the task as you are, can be a challenge.

Here are some potential motivators:

Sources of motivation

What other sources would you add from your own experience? Perhaps it is having a comfortable place to work, or the opportunity to be of service.

The degree of motivation you feel may in part depend on how long you have been working in the same role or within the same organisation. People are usually enthusiastic when starting out on a new job or a new project, and keen to get the most out of the opportunity, but without nurturing, motivation can wane. Having your strengths, qualities and

---

[5] Daniel H. Pink, *Drive – the surprising truth about what motivates us*, Canongate Books, 2011.

skills recognised and appreciated is a powerful motivator – and the inverse is true, few things can be more discouraging and de-motivating than the sense of being taken for granted or overlooked.

Much that is written about motivation suggests that the nurturing of motivation will be a one-direction initiative from the leader or manager to their team. The fact is that you can't *make* someone motivated – motivation comes from within the person themselves. As Marilyn Ferguson said, *'Each of us guards a gate of change that can only be opened from the inside.'* Certainly, the manager or leader can set the tone for an environment where team members can flourish, but that culture will only thrive when all team members take full responsibility for motivating themselves too!

So let's begin by thinking about personal motivators and think about how you can contribute to creating an environment in which everyone is able to maintain – and restore when necessary – their *own* level of motivation and thereby perhaps also create the environment that motivates their leader/manager.

Three men were working in a quarry. They spent all day breaking up rocks.

Workman A
Q   'What are you doing?'
A   In a resentful voice, 'I'm breaking up rocks all day.'

Workman B
Q   'What are you doing?'
A   In a compliant voice, 'I'm breaking up rocks – I think they're going to be used to build a wall.'

Workman C
Q   'What are you doing?'
A   Replies positively, 'I'm breaking up rocks – and these same rocks are going to be used to build a cathedral!'

Who do you think found most enjoyment in their work? Why?

Understanding more about motivation

Many theories seek to explain the sources of motivation – and therefore how it can be encouraged and maintained. For most people, personal values such as creativity, justice, service, harmony and excellence are powerful motivators, especially (as we mentioned in Chapter 7) when the organisation shares these values. A work culture where this alignment is absent de-motivates and encourages cynicism and inertia; ultimately this disconnection is a common reason why people leave their organisations.

In the early 1940s psychologist Abraham Maslow presented his ideas about human motivation in his 'Theory of Needs'.[1] His premise is that human behaviour at its most essential level is motivated by physiological needs and the need for safety and security. Once these needs have been satisfied, other important needs – for belonging, esteem and self-actualisation – can then be addressed.

In the following table we show Maslow's five needs and we give examples of each of these needs:

Five needs	Examples of these needs
Self-actualisation needs and transcendence	Achieving one's full potential, including creative activities, giving of oneself beyond oneself, e.g. being of service to others, and spirituality
Self-esteem needs	Respect, status, freedom, self-esteem

---

[1] Abraham Maslow, *A theory of human motivation*, Wilder Publications, 2013 (first published 1943).

Social belonging needs	Friendships, family, intimacy, sense of connection, inclusion
Safety needs	Security, safety, employment, property, stability
Physiological needs	Food, water, warmth, rest, clothing, health

Maslow's hierarchy of needs (adapted)

The belief that humans need their safety and physiological needs met before they can consider their higher needs is obviously not universally true. You can, no doubt, look back through history and think of composers, artists, mystics and religious leaders who focused solely on higher-level needs, often at the cost of their security and health.

What drives us at work?

Over the decades Maslow's hierarchy has been re-interpreted and re-imagined many times over, for different contexts and different audiences.

Working for over 25 years with hundreds of managers worldwide we frequently facilitate sessions on motivation. We ask participants to assume that they are satisfied that their employer meets their physiological and safety needs. We then ask two questions: 'What gets you out of bed on a dark, wet weekday morning?' and 'What specific aspects of your work do you find particularly motivating?' When summarising the replies to these two questions we find that most of the participants are motivated by one of these two drivers:

Driver A – Focused on tasks and completing them to a high standard. This person likes to be seen as the expert and to be given challenging technical work. The worst thing you can do to this person is to humiliate them when they do not know the answer to a technical point

Driver B – Focused on people, particularly their own team members. This person is sociable and enjoys being part of the team. The worst thing you can do to this person is to (accidentally) omit them from a team event or meeting

A smaller number of participants are represented by:

Driver C – Focused on influential people, e.g. senior management, their peers and key external stakeholders. They like to be 'seen' and want to be involved in important projects and business development events, even when these are the responsibility of other people. The worst thing you can do to this person is to ignore or exclude them.

If you would like to look at each of these drivers in greater detail, there is a link at the end of this chapter.

It seems that these three drivers are installed in us in our early years and that one of them usually develops into being stronger than the other two. One is not more important than the others and they are not related to your intelligence or competence. Our main driver probably does not change significantly over time. What we can do is to become more aware of the effect of our drivers on other people who may be motivated differently. We can then choose to modify our behaviour to reduce the impact of a particularly strong driver and/or to build up a weak driver.

As we discussed when talking about personalities in Chapter 3, the different drivers bring different gifts to the overall performance of the team. In the ideal world each team should have at least one person who is dominant in each driver, and certainly they should recognise the consequences of an imbalance.

Personal reflection

What is your dominant driver? Are your needs being sufficiently met? If you have a strong driver does this get in the way of delegating your work? If so, we pick up this point in Chapter 12.

Some years ago, we worked with the managers of a global technology company and facilitated workshops on motivation at each of their major locations. We found that no matter which continent we visited, each office had a similar profile, i.e. their highest driver was Driver B, followed by Driver A, and lagging well behind in third place was Driver C. It was while we were working with this company that they acquired a smaller global technology company which was sales-led. Their motivation profile was noticeably different. Their highest driver was Driver C, followed by Driver A, with Driver B in third place. Our work on motivation post-acquisition helped everyone to understand why there was friction between the two sets of managers. This friction eased when they began to appreciate the benefits that each of the three drivers brought to the party and how they could choose to modify their behaviour to soften the impact of any particularly strong driver.

Allocating work and giving feedback

Don't judge each day by the harvest you reap but by the seeds you plant.

(Robert Louis Stevenson)

You may find the following useful when delegating work or giving feedback to colleagues who seem to have a high preference for one of these drivers.

Driver A

Team members who are motivated primarily by Driver A need challenging, but not impossible, projects that they can see will help the organisation achieve its vision and strategies. They thrive on overcoming difficult problems or situations, so make sure you keep them engaged this way. They work very effectively either alone or with other high achievers. When providing feedback, give them a rational and balanced appraisal. They want to know what they're doing right and how they can improve.

Driver B

They work best in a group environment, so whenever possible try to integrate them with a team (versus working alone). When providing feedback to these people, be personal. It's still important to give balanced feedback, but if you start your appraisal by emphasising their good working relationships and your trust in them, they'll likely be more open to what else you want to say. Remember that these people often don't want to stand out, so it might be best to praise them in private rather than in front of others.

Driver C

They work best when they're in charge. Because they enjoy competition, they do well with goal-oriented projects or tasks. They may also be very effective in negotiations or in situations in which another party must be persuaded of an idea or goal. When providing feedback, be direct and action-orientated with these team members. Encourage them to focus their competitive spirit on the external competition, not on their colleagues, and keep them motivated by helping them further their career goals.

Motivating Generation Y

Do you work with Millennials – or are you a Millennial yourself? Much has been said and written over the last ten years or so about the issues around working with Millennials – that is, people born between the early 1980s and the mid-1990s, often referred to as Generation Y. Of course, each generation brings new ideas to the team and encounters new challenges based on innovations in all fields and changing educational and professional landscapes – and the next generation entering the workforce generally receives some complaints too! However, the fact is that Generation Y are the new or future managers and leaders so it's important to think about how their assumptions and aspirations can impact on motivation.

Millennials' familiarity with digital technology has opened up for them new possibilities and perspectives on the world, including the world of work. They are accustomed to negotiation, want to be involved and generally think that 'no' is not a satisfactory answer – so ownership and influence determine the degree of motivation and commitment much more than in previous generations. More significantly many Millennials also want to feel inspired at work and tend to set significant importance on feeling happy and fulfilled.

There are noticeable differences in the assumptions and expectations of Millennials and Generation Z (1995–2002) and previous generations:

> ➢ They are technology-savvy and readily get instant access to the knowledge they need. They also make full use of their social media network for support and

to get things done. These two elements combined mean that they tend to be flexible and to have (and expect) a more autonomous way of working

➢ They also want to be involved and expect to have their ideas listened to and taken seriously – and may sometimes be impatient if this does not happen early in their working life

➢ They tend to focus on 'higher order' needs (as in Maslow's hierarchy of needs), wanting a sense of purpose and meaning to the work they do, and this early in their career. Previous generations had typically focused on 'lower order' needs, with life purpose perhaps coming into focus later in their work-life

➢ They will often be less inclined to wait for the 'deferred rewards' accepted as a principle by earlier generations – and their expectation of rapid promotion can cause tension with more senior colleagues

➢ They expect to receive regular feedback, while at the same time not appreciating micro-management

It could be argued that by paying attention to the motivational needs of Millennials everyone will benefit. Most people want to be successful, fulfilled and happy in their work, to be appreciated for the value they bring to their organisation and to have a good work-life balance. Rather belatedly we could thank Millennials for raising the bar for all employees. Aligning the culture of your work environment with deep, human motivations should have a positive impact on employee engagement, making people across all generations more content and successful.

Conclusion

> When everything seems to be going against you, remember that the airplane takes off against the wind, not with it.
>
> (Henry Ford)

By now you will have realised in this and in other chapters that you and each of your colleagues are unique human beings and therefore need different factors to help you feel self-motivated and willing 'to go the extra mile' (also known as 'discretionary effort'). Understanding the basics of motivation will help you realise what strategies work best for you. It will also help you to use different ways to help increase your team members' levels of motivation. This chapter contains many ideas on how you might create a motivational environment for yourself and for your colleagues.

You have a right to spend time ensuring your own level of motivation; self-care is not selfish when its aim is to improve relationships and performance. It will help if you gravitate towards colleagues who are self-motivated. If you believe in what you do, this will show in the way you behave each day, and your team members can feed off that.

If you have a manager role or are in a position to influence your team's thinking, here are some prompts to help create a motivating atmosphere for yourself and your team:

> ➢ If the team's level of motivation seems to be low, first examine your own level of motivation. If it is low this may be the cause of the problem. It is worth remembering the old saying *'Enthusiasm is contagious and so is the lack of it'*

> ➢ Remember that motivation is only one aspect of work performance – be careful not to use 'lack

of motivation' as a blanket explanation for poor performance

➢ Review each of the levels of Maslow's hierarchy of needs. Which points, when strengthened, would have a positive impact on motivation?

➢ Everyday contacts with colleagues, including when delegating and giving feedback, are opportunities for the recipients to boost their levels of motivation

➢ Just as you are aware how your line manager's character and their levels of motivation affect you, your colleagues are also noticing and are affected by your character and levels of motivation

➢ In the case of a long-term project:

➢ Break down the project into smaller packages of work, review each completed package before moving on to the next stage. These interim deadlines and reviews can help maintain a high level of motivation

➢ At the start of a long-term project agree with the client that a different person will be seconded to the client at the beginning of each new stage. This can provide the project with a fresh impetus and help colleagues maintain their level of motivation during their periods of secondment

➢ Checking-in is even more important with colleagues you do not see every week. They need to be reminded that they are not forgotten, are still very much part of the team and that their contribution is noted and valued. We refer to this more fully in Chapter 13

➤ Motivation is not just about goals and tasks. It is also about encouraging behaviours and attitudes that are consistent with organisational goals and values. Rewarding those behaviours and attitudes – in various ways – acknowledges their importance in underpinning the values of the organisation

➤ Create a culture of 'we' and 'us' in the team. A team will never be a completely homogeneous group but creating one that ensures a sense of belonging and promotes trust will foster a culture where colleagues feel motivated and can develop to their full potential

Applying this to your workplace

a) Write down the top 3–5 things that motivate you and think creatively how you might meet these needs more frequently in your day-to-day work

b) How might reframing what you do increase your level of motivation? Think about the ultimate outcome of the work you do, e.g. 'I help save people's lives' rather than 'I maintain electrical equipment at the local hospital' seems to be more motivating

c) Find out more about your personal motivators by visiting www.learningcorporation.co.uk/Library and downloading further information

d) Think about a colleague with whom you work closely and who you think probably has different motivators to yours. What is their main driver? Make a note of your answers to the following questions:

➤ How could your different main drivers be beneficial when you work together?

> ➤ How might you annoy each other and what aspects of the work might be overlooked?

> ➤ How could you 'contract' with each other to overcome any difficulties?

e) Consider completing our Team Performance Assessment and review the results in the context of increasing individual and/or the team's current level of motivation. A copy of this form can be found at www.learningcorporation.co.uk/Library

Further references

> ➤ Jacobs, Susanne, *Drivers: creating trust and motivation at work*, Panoma Press, 2017

> ➤ Pink, Dan, *Drive: the surprising truth about what motivates us*, Canongate Books, 2011

> ➤ Ryan, R. M. and Deci, E. L., 'Self-determination theory and the facilitation of intrinsic motivation, social development, and well-being', *American Psychologist*, 55(1), 68–78, 2000

> ➤ Sirota, David, Mischkind, Louis and Meltzer, Michael, *The enthusiastic employee: how companies profit by giving workers what they want: what employees want and why employers should give it to them*, Financial Times/Prentice Hall, 2005

10

My best self: making the most of my strengths

Hide not your talents. They for use were made.
What's a sundial in the shade?

(Benjamin Franklin)

Introduction

Have you ever been to a school/workplace reunion, years after you left, and met up with an old colleague who you really liked and who you haven't seen for ages? Perhaps you hardly recognised them, with their changed hairstyle and older-looking face. But once you got talking to them again, within five minutes you realised, 'This person hasn't changed at all! – Their concern for people, or their ability to analyse, or their attention to detail or their capacity to see the big picture... They haven't changed at all over the years.'

Your unique core strengths and qualities are part of your core make-up and set you apart from thousands of other people. Once you realise your unique talents and strengths, you will know better what will give you the most job satisfaction and stimulus in the long run – and what may let you down if over-used.

We're not talking about how to develop your skills or competences. Through technical training, over time, you can learn how to do many tasks well, but that doesn't necessarily mean that they will give you deep personal satisfaction or a sense of fulfilment. You may get asked time and time again to carry out the same sort of work because your manager thinks it plays to one of your strengths, but you know that what your manager sees as one of your talents or strengths may in fact be a learned behaviour. Your core strengths have been with you for most of your life and are very deeply wired – in a good way, if you know how to use them wisely, which is what we want to talk about in this chapter.

In this chapter we are keen to share with you:

➤ the benefits of identifying your top 2–4 unique talents and strengths and being intentional about how you use them

➤ the idea of focusing more on your strengths than on your weaknesses, in your development

➤ the danger of over-using your talents and strengths as this may cause problems with your relationships

Our experience has demonstrated that focusing on strengths rather than weaknesses has a significant impact on individuals and teams in the workplace. Typically, people feel happier and more confident, less stressed and more resilient. Other benefits include:

➤ higher self-esteem and a stronger sense of identity

➤ increased energy and vitality

➤ greater sense of perspective and clarity about the choices they make

> ➢ improved performance

> ➢ greater satisfaction, fulfilment and engagement

> ➢ higher staff retention

Why focus on strengths?

In the 1980s, work on 'Appreciative Enquiry' suggested that individuals and teams can develop more effectively if they focus on what is working well. During the same period a 'Solution Focus' approach suggested that focusing on what we want (solution) rather than what we don't want (problem) and finding out what works well for us and how to build on what works well is the most effective way of fostering success and achieving excellence.

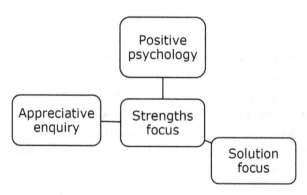

The origins of recent work on strengths

Then in the late 1990s an American psychologist, Martin Seligman,[1] started a movement known as Positive Psychology. Seligman has been an avid promoter within the scientific community of the field of Positive Psychology, not

---

[1] Martin Seligman, *Learned optimism*, Pocket Books, 1998.

simply because he has a systematic theory about why happy people are happy, but because he uses a scientific method to explore it. Using exhaustive questionnaires, Seligman found that the most satisfied, positive and fulfilled people were those who had discovered and exploited their unique combination of 'signature strengths'.

Strengths as source of energy

According to Paul Brewerton and James Brook,[2] *'Strengths are the underlying qualities that energise you, contribute to personal growth and lead to peak performance.'* Think about those times when everything is going well at work – you're at the top of your game, you are 'in flow', getting things done, loving every minute and enjoying yourself. At these times you're not just doing what you're good at – you're thriving and energised – even if you're feeling tired, you're more likely to be feeling invigorated than exhausted.

When you're playing to your strengths, you have a sense of ownership and authenticity ('This is really me') and a feeling of excitement while displaying it, particularly at first. Consciously or unconsciously you'll be looking for new ways of using your strengths – creating personal projects that revolve around them and experiencing a general joy, buzz and enthusiasm while using them. Even learning new stuff seems to take less effort so you'll be eager to find new opportunities to use and explore these strengths.[3]

---

[2] Brook, James and Brewerton, Paul, *Strengthscope®* handbook: your guide to achieving success through optimising strengths and reducing performance risks, Matador, 2018.

[3] Martin Seligman, *Authentic happiness*, Nicholas Brealey, 2002.

How to identify your core strengths

If you:

> ➤ invest some time to identify your unique talents and strengths; and

> ➤ use these talents and strengths as often as possible at work and in your private life,

you will feel that you are living a more fulfilling life, especially if your efforts are in the service of others, e.g. your clients, family and community.

For example, the first half of my career was as a chartered accountant during which time I acquired fabulous experience working with small and global organisations in, for example, accounting, acquisitions, strategy, company turnarounds, business development, marketing and selling, in over 20 countries and in virtually every industry group. I was a competent employee and was promoted accordingly. Later I unearthed my top three unique talents which shape the second part of my career and which energise me. They are:

Talent/strength	Examples of activities that give me great satisfaction
Creator Builder Enabler/ Encourager	Creating a pan-European firm, the Guildford Business Forum, Guildford Job Club; advising 60+ business start-ups; writing articles and books to help others; facilitating countless workshops, coaching and mentoring; creating a 39-mile circular walk around Guildford, a jazz club, two chamber choirs, two small singing groups, my walking group.

For easy steps on how to explore your uniqueness and discover your unique strengths and talents see *Creating a purposeful life*.[4] As a starting point you could use a list of possible strengths we have prepared. To obtain a copy of this list please see the link at the end of this chapter.

Your strengths can become a liability

O would some Power the gift give us
To see ourselves as others see us.

(Robert Burns)

It's hard to imagine that strengths that can be so positive and so energising can sometimes go awry. Have you ever come across a work colleague who is impatient or arrogant or pushy, or who fusses or nags? Their behaviour may be because they are over-using one of their strengths. If this over-use becomes a habit it is likely to damage working relationships.

Sometimes a strength can be our greatest performance risk if...

➢   we use it in the wrong situation

➢   with the wrong person...

➢   or just use it too much!

Strengths in overdrive

Especially when we are under pressure, feeling over-stretched or under exceptional stress we can risk 'overdoing' our strengths. Here are a few examples:

---

[4] Richard Fox and Heather Brown, *Creating a purposeful life – how to reclaim your life, live more meaningfully and befriend time*, Infinite Ideas, 2012.

Strength	→	Likely results of an over-used strength
Autonomous	→	Detached from the team – no longer aware of the needs of others
Committed	→	Workaholic, setting impossibly high standards, over-tired, irritable
Careful, prudent	→	Requesting more and more data, reluctant, incapable of independent decision-making, procrastinating
Decisive	→	Pushy, disempowering, impatient, controlling
Visionary	→	Unable to focus on one thing, give directions or follow anything through to completion
Results-focused	→	Steamrollering others, running from one result to the next, over-driven to the point of burn-out
Helpful or caring	→	Interfering, fussing, overbearing, feeling like some sort of parent–child relationship

To cope with stressful situations, the temptation is to return to the strengths we know we have – and just do them more, rather like turning up the volume. However, excessive pulling on our favourite strengths in this way can have the opposite effect, both on the individual and the team. What then tends to happen is that we get some form of feedback – sometimes quite forceful feedback – that the other person does not like our behaviour. You may have heard words like 'Stop micro-managing me', 'Why do you need to plan so far ahead?'

Handling this feedback

The big question then is how to handle this type of feedback. Some people, who are particularly self-aware, can spot when they are about to over-use a strength and can pull back and adjust their behaviour. Others can modify their behaviour themselves... eventually.

Then there are others who decide to withdraw completely and say to themselves something like, 'OK, if you don't want me to help you, you can get on with the job yourself.' These people become stuck in a state of withdrawal/abdication; their strengths are denied, and they become shut off from their true self. This emotional state does not feel at all comfortable to the person who has received the feedback, as abdicating responsibility is not something that this person really wants to do. It also puzzles other members of the team and they might feel abandoned.

Without an opportunity to revisit their own personal development needs, perhaps through coaching, or moving into a different role/team, they may even experience some sort of crisis – an uncharacteristic explosion of emotion ('Nobody appreciates me'), a health breakdown, or feelings of being unable to manage the job. They may simply decide to leave the organisation, taking their unresolved behavioural problem with them.

Finding balance

Should you find yourself in an uncomfortable position as a result of over-using your strengths, we suggest that you focus first on being clear about your strengths, so that you can start from a position of confidence, grounded in your authentic self. Then think about what these strengths might look, sound and feel like when over-used. From there, perhaps with some coaching support, you can find a more balanced way of being and behaving that you will be happy with and that would also work well with your colleagues.

The overall experience looks something like this:

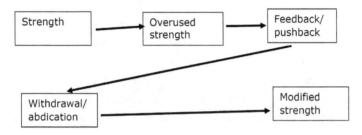

How an over-used strength can rebound on the individual and those around them

Reflecting on your strengths when handling difficult relationships

Think about a work colleague or client who you don't get on with so well, with whom communication is difficult, or who simply winds you up! You can learn a lot about yourself from those you find most difficult to interact with – what irritates you in someone else may well be an excess of a strength you also possess. For example, you may secretly like to be the centre of attention and you may be bristling at the energetic new colleague who now is always stealing the limelight. (In Chapter 7 we look at a related concept called 'Projection'.)

Or your colleague's strength may the opposite to yours. Here are some examples:

> ➤ If you are decisive you may find it hard to tolerate a colleague you regard as passive

> ➢ If you are flexible you may be irritated by another's apparent rigidity

> ➢ If you are overtly warm and empathetic you may be critical of the aloofness in your colleague's apparent detachment

Once you have identified what is happening you are better able to understand the other person's behaviour and respond more appropriately.

So far in this chapter we have focused primarily on the impact of one person's behaviour on another individual. In practice it is quite likely that more than one person in a department is over-using their strengths, creating a more complicated system. An experienced facilitator in systemic team-working can help the whole team understand what is going on and how to overcome the tensions in working relationships.

What about weaknesses?

There often seems to be a bit of an obsession with focusing on what's going wrong rather than what's going right, what you're not good at rather than what you shine at. Perhaps you are someone who mainly receives feedback about what you need to improve? (We talk more about feedback in Chapter 11.)

A strengths focus doesn't ignore weaknesses but asks the question: 'Is this a performance risk? – Does not having this strength adversely affect my ability to do a good job or does it have a negative impact on my relationships within the team?' If it presents no serious problem to performance or to working relationships in the team it can be considered an allowable weakness. Indeed, your weakness might turn out to be a strength. For example, someone who might describe themselves as a bit of a worrier may have found over the years that mulling things over enables solutions to pop up almost unbidden. For this person, this apparent weakness has become a strength and a key to success.

No one can possess all the strengths in equal measure, but focusing exclusively on weaknesses simply leads, with many people, to reduced energy, low levels of motivation, and poorer performance. Instead think about how you can make more of the strengths you are currently under-using.

Conclusion

It is worth repeating that if you want to make a real positive difference in your organisation and/or community we encourage you to first discover your innate, unique strengths and then find ways to use them regularly, especially in the service of others – your colleagues, clients, family and community.

Just imagine the positive impact on productivity and well-being if all your colleagues knew their 2–4 top unique talents and strengths and their job descriptions were reshaped so that they could regularly use their strengths.

Finally, think of the positive impact on motivation if performance reviews and day-to-day feedback focused more on specific things that you and your colleagues are doing particularly well, rather than on minor slip-ups.

Applying this to your workplace

a) We find that people, even in senior positions, do not know their unique talents and strengths. So, think about a time when everything was going well at work – when you were 'at the top of your game' and really enjoying what you were doing. What personal strengths did you use that made things go smoothly? How can you adjust your role or the type of work you do so that you use this strength more frequently?

b) In order to help identify your top strengths and talents you can obtain a long list of possible strengths by going to www.learningcorporation.co.uk/Library and downloading a copy

c) Also on the website is a case study you may like to study on the consequences of over-using a strength

d) Think about a time when you were really under pressure at work. If this caused you to overplay one of your strengths what did that look and sound like to others? What sort of thing would you like to say to yourself to pull yourself back from the brink? How might colleagues help you (and you help them) at times like this? What would you like to do in order to modify this strength? What would be the benefits to you and others?

e) Thinking about your career in the medium to longer term and the threat to your career of AI, robotics and other technology, what strengths should you develop to future-proof your employability against these imminent threats?

Further references

> Brook, James and Brewerton, Paul, *Strengthscope® handbook: your guide to achieving success through optimising strengths and reducing performance risks*, Matador, 2018

> Csikszentmihalyi, Mihaly, *Flow: the psychology of happiness*, Rider, 2002

➢ Fox, Richard and Brown, Heather, *Creating a purposeful life – how to reclaim your life, live more meaningfully and befriend time*, Infinite Ideas, 2012

➢ Linley, A., Willars, J. and Biswas-Diener, R., *The strengths book*, CAPP Press, 2010

➢ Seligman, Martin, *Flourish: a new understanding of happiness and well-being*, Nicholas Brealey, 2011

11

The art of good feedback: feedback for learning

There is no failure, only feedback and an opportunity for learning.

Introduction

Here are some comments we have heard from clients:

I have been working here for eight months and I haven't got a clue how I'm getting on. Hopefully, silence means good news... or does it?

At my performance review two weeks before Christmas my boss told me something he had heard from a director about my performance back in February. I don't really know what I was supposed to have done wrong. Why wasn't this raised with me last February?

We were working long days on an intensive project. Late on Thursday evening the project manager asked me to stay behind to talk about an incident that happened earlier that day. I was angry because I was tired, and it takes me over an hour to get home. Surely the meeting could have waited.

We would all agree that these are examples of how not to give feedback. So, what is good feedback and how can you improve your ability to give and receive it? This chapter focuses first on how to give feedback, and then talks about how to receive it.

What is the aim of feedback?

Feedback is an opportunity to recognise good work, discuss specific areas for improvement, show appreciation, offer support, encourage and motivate. Feedback is imperative to staff satisfaction, working effectively and achieving high performance. But in a more general sense, setting up a system and an organisational culture to give and receive good feedback will have enormous benefits for team-working, levels of trust and general motivation. It's about more than just regular review, it's about creating a culture of reflective practice.

Encouraging a culture of reflective practice

Reflective practice is where everyone (team members and managers) reviews their own performance on a regular basis, celebrates their own strengths and achievements and identifies areas where improvement and support are needed. This approach means that problems can be identified sooner and remedied without a feeling of fear, in a spirit of collaborative continuous improvement.

You may not be in a management role, but everyone has responsibility for building a culture of honesty and openness. If you are a manager you can set a great example of reflective practice by inviting regular feedback from your line manager, peers and team members. State what you're personally working on, the changes you're trying to make and encourage and invite feedback on the progress you're making.

The feedback questions you ask yourself and others can be very simple and straightforward, for example:

What was good/did you value about the way I...?

What advice would you give me for my development?

Asking this second question of others is a challenge for most of us, because we don't know what we're going to hear. Before you ask the question, take a couple of deep breaths and feel your feet firm on the ground. Relax your shoulders and make good eye contact (if that's appropriate in your culture). Be curious about how the other person sees the world and your work. The benefit of a feedback conversation is not just about the information we hear; it's an opportunity to build openness and trust in your relationship with the person giving it – there is a longer-term benefit.

You may feel that you don't have time to do this reflection and requesting feedback on a regular basis. But ask yourself the questions:

What might be the benefits for me and for the team of doing this?

What might be the consequences of not doing it?

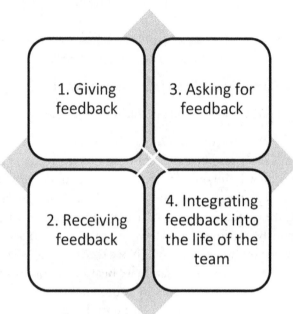

1. Giving feedback

3. Asking for feedback

2. Receiving feedback

4. Integrating feedback into the life of the team

Feedback – a cycle of reflection, learning and change

Feedback as part of a regular review cycle

To have the best impact – on the individual and on the team – feedback needs to be integrated into the everyday life of the team as a cycle of reflection, learning and change. If you have management responsibilities you can start the ball rolling by:

➤ reviewing your own practice regularly – both the tasks you have achieved and the relationships you have built

➤ setting up opportunities for reflective practice with your teams, for example, adding an agenda item at the end of meetings to invite attendees to give feedback on how you chaired the meeting, or about how the team worked together during the meeting; this doesn't need to happen at every meeting, but it does need to happen regularly and be given quality time in the meeting

➢ asking for feedback from your manager – and from your direct reports

Most organisations have appraisal systems which mean that feedback is delivered regularly. It is often accompanied by a 360° report, which means that feedback can be quite formalised, involving forms, answering questions and even numerical evaluations of a person's performance. While numerical data appeals to some people's learning styles, it can be the source of arguments such as 'Why did you give me a 4 and not a 5?', which can lead to tension. The ideal is to get a balance which makes the feedback session feel more like a reflective review: 'Where is the organisation trying to get to?' 'What is your role within that?' 'Let's reflect together on how the last period has gone for you.'

Good quality feedback, modelled by leaders and replicated within the team as part of normal working practice, encourages an open culture of learning and a culture of candour rather than a culture of blame. This kind of conversation provides an opportunity for increasing the level of desire for improvement. This will also encourage a mind-set for learning and continuous professional development which will benefit the individual and the whole team.

The purpose and benefits of good feedback

The purpose and benefits of feedback include:

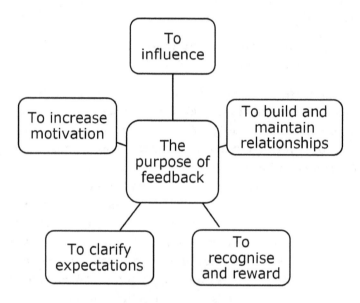

> ➤ Good quality feedback builds constructive relationships, helps teams achieve their objectives and supports continuing professional development

> ➤ Giving regular feedback helps to create an open climate, where trust and support is a mutual expectation and where the focus is on personal and team responsibility and creating a culture of continuous learning

> ➤ Clear and timely performance feedback gives clarity about the 'what, how, why and when' of individual

roles and tasks and improves the quality of the work of the team. Team members need clear and unambiguous information to help them meet expectations about doing the job well

➤ Positive feedback is powerful – recognising the efforts that your colleagues are making and rewarding that effort with appreciation mean that they are more likely to perform well. Be specific: 'That was great' and 'Well done' is always welcome, but 'I just wanted to tell you how much I appreciated the way you...' or 'This is a really an outstanding piece of work' and then telling the person specifically what it is that makes it excellent. This shows that they have really been 'seen' carrying out a task particularly well, communicating effectively, or demonstrating a skill or expertise

➤ Use feedback to clarify expectations and so prevent guesswork about performance. People are more likely to meet your expectations if you give accurate information about what is appreciated, needed and valued, and what isn't. Given challenging feedback, people are more likely to be motivated to change if you show that you have seen, heard and understood them – and you are offering to support them as they change

The role and purpose of feedback needs to be established right at the beginning of the working relationship, when a new member joins the team. This could be part of the 'contracting' process we talked about in Chapter 7.

How not to do feedback

Even well-intentioned feedback can go wrong. Let's look at this example of a conversation between Blair and his manager Casey after Blair had delivered a client presentation:

How lack of preparation – on both sides – can derail a feedback conversation

How did the exchange about Blair's client presentation deteriorate so quickly? Casey isn't that far away from Blair in her view of how the presentation went. However, as egos become inflated and each tries to pull the other into their way of thinking, they both move further away from an opportunity for appreciation and learning – and closer to a complete breakdown in communication. At the end of this conversation it's very unlikely that Blair had gained any kind of insight or increased self-awareness.

Had both parties previously developed a shared understanding about feedback and its purpose? Did Casey make her expectations – and those of the client – clear to Blair so that he would know what a 'good job' looked like, and they would have a shared reference point against which to judge the quality of Blair's work?

Pause for reflection

Before you read the following sections, you might like to think about what you would have done differently... in either role...

The process of giving feedback effectively

Most people understand the term 'giving feedback' as implying some kind of hierarchy where the giver is in the more powerful position. When preparing to give feedback in normal circumstances (i.e. not in disciplinary circumstances) it's good to neutralise the sense of hierarchy as much as possible.

Preparing to give feedback

➢ Choose the right time and place; five minutes in a corridor or a rushed exchange at the end of a tiring day will undermine the best of intentions. Choose somewhere quiet where you will not be interrupted, and set aside enough time not to feel rushed. Make sure that seating is comfortable and arranged in a way that is conducive to an open conversation

➤ Think about the context of the conversation and be aware of the importance of power dynamics, cultural influences (educational, gender, professional, national, religious...) which impact on the conversation. It can be a good idea to address these openly at the beginning of the conversation

➤ Be clear about your intentions: the outcome you want by the end of the conversation. Think about how you want the content to be understood, but also think about what you want your relationship with the person to be like at the end of the conversation

➤ Think about how you will build trust and make it safe to talk. How can you build trust before the conversation, so that they don't feel anxious or threatened when receiving feedback (refer to Chapter 2 for suggestions about building trust right from the start of the relationship)

➤ Use your EQ: think about the kinds of emotions that might be present in the room. Be aware of your own assumptions, biases and distortions, 'hot buttons' and vulnerabilities. How will you manage yourself in order to stay present and value the good things about your colleague?

➤ Think about how the feedback conversation can be most effective, based on (a) your knowledge of the team member through your 1 to 1 observations, and

(b) what you know about the team member's own style and their work preferences. How will you take account of their preferences and build rapport? (See Chapters 2 and 3)

➤ Gather the specific documents together that you want to discuss

➤ Develop a logical, structured approach in order to ensure that all the key steps are covered in the conversation. This also helps to maintain consistency between conversations and gives a feeling of pace and focus. For example, we tend to use BROFF in our professional work. BROFF stands for **B**ehaviour; **R**easons; **O**utcome; **F**eelings; **F**uture. For an example of a feedback conversation using the BROFF process please refer to the link at the end of this chapter

➤ Ensure that feedback is never a personal attack

➤ Think about how you can place most of the emphasis of the conversation on the future instead of the past. After all, you can't do anything about the past, but you hope your feedback will improve the future. If the idea of feedforward appeals to you, look up the reference at the end of this chapter

Make sure that as you prepare, you have their best interest at heart – and mean it. Plan to open the feedback conversation by stating this in some way, and by ensuring that you keep the meeting a two-way conversation.

A caveat about the feedback sandwich – handle with care! Change 'but' to 'and' for increased trust and effectiveness...

"Don't take this the wrong way, but..."

Feedback is often delivered – with the best of intentions – in a sandwich form:

> ➤ positive appreciation for work done well

> ➤ delivery of bad news

> ➤ attempt to end on a positive note

However, if you start with positive appreciation, most people will be listening for the BUT which they expect to follow it. The person receiving this feedback will typically only remember what was said after BUT, which focuses attention on what hasn't worked well or still needs to be improved.

You can change the tone of the whole conversation by simply using 'and' instead of 'but'. It will sound weird at first – persevere and you'll notice the difference:

I really appreciate the way you started the presentation. You really captured the client's attention AND next time I think you could maintain the high energy level you created by... What do you think?

A word about criticism

Giving feedback makes many people uneasy, particularly when they need to address an issue relating to under-performance.

What if they take it the wrong way? Will this destroy our working relationship? A positive and non-judgemental intention is the essential starting point in preventing people hearing what you say as damaging and unhelpful 'criticism'. Criticism is about giving negative or judgemental messages – that's not what good feedback is about. Your intention should be to be helpful, to focus on the behaviour and not the person, to be future-focused, to use your experience to help the other person improve and grow.

Starting the feedback conversation

Feedback conversations should provide structured information about the individual's way of working, their performance, their communication style and their contribution to the team. During the conversation you will be able to find out if your colleague has the knowledge and skills and, most importantly, the desire to make the changes needed to further their professional development and capability.

Feedback is a two-way conversation. Your aim may be to praise past work and/or identify areas for improvement, but the first thing you need to do is establish trust and openness.

It is important to ask a few open questions to get the dialogue going:

So how are things going?

or:

How have things been going since our last conversation?

During this part of the conversation, find a way to ask your colleague to give themselves feedback about their progress or performance – they may say a lot of the things you were going to say to them, which will make your job much easier. Listen carefully and value what they say (i.e. don't start thinking about the feedback you are about to give). You may find out more than you knew this way, and/or realise that your preoccupations are the same as those of your colleague.

Discussing specific feedback points

> The best conversations are as much about listening as talking. Allow time and opportunity for the other person to think and reflect. Make full use of your 'active listening' skills (see Chapter 6)

> Be specific – make sure feedback is based on objective facts and observations

> Aim for clarity, neutrality and moderation; avoid generalising, distorting and deleting (see Chapter 4)

> Do not criticise the person themselves, or their 'attitude' – this is a subjective judgement and will only make them defensive

> Take a non-judgemental position; don't get into right or wrong, or the blame game. When people feel judged, they are likely to shut down and become defensive, so stay objective and constructive. State observations not interpretations

> Help the person to understand more about their own personality and who they are, and help your colleague to formulate their own ideas for moving forward by asking open questions such as:

>> 'What would "success" look like to you?'

> ➤ 'How would you go about achieving that next time?'

> ➤ 'What do you want/need to do next?'

> ➤ 'What support might you need to make this happen?'

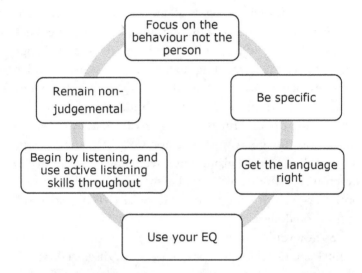

Planning for the future

There are several things you can do now to maximise the benefit to both parties of the conversation you are having. Here are some general principles:

> ➤ Make sure that you have agreed a shared plan/ decision/list of options, etc. before the end of the meeting

> ➤ Thank the other person for their contribution to the meeting

> ➤ Send a positively worded email within a couple of days of the meeting, summarising key points/action plan with agreed dates

> ➢ Don't let the conversation or the relationship go 'cold' – e.g. organise, if wanted, additional support promptly and talk again soon – formally or informally

Manage your expectations

One feedback session every 6–12 months will not necessarily be the spark for instant insight or dramatic change. Feedback needs to be part of a cycle rather than a one-off exchange – it is the start of a coaching/mentoring relationship which includes follow-up, consolidation, actionable targets, change and more learning as part of a continuous professional development plan. Practise giving feedback as often as you can – both for good work and for work that needs to be improved. You'll be giving your team the opportunity to practise receiving it too – and remember, feedback works both ways, so think about how you receive feedback as well as how you deliver it.

So now you're ready to put these ideas into action. Here's a quick summary of the points we have discussed, which will help you create an effective culture where feedback is welcomed and used positively.

> ➢ Demonstrate how feedback can be part of normal practice in the team – a two-way face-to-face conversation which encourages no-blame, non-judgemental learning for the benefit of the individual and the whole team

> ➢ Plan – think about what you are trying to achieve through the feedback conversation and choose an appropriate time and place

> ➢ Acknowledge your colleague's contribution to the work of the team and the strengths, qualities

and expertise they demonstrate in their role – be specific, descriptive and objective

➤ Keep your focus on helping them make decisions about changing their behaviour and improving their performance in the future – end with an agreed shared plan for moving forward

Asking for feedback

We stated at the beginning of the chapter that it's important to proactively seek feedback – for your own well-being and professional integrity and the effectiveness of the whole team.

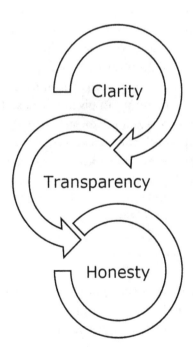

Asking for feedback may be difficult at first, but be clear about your own expectations. If what you would really like is just appreciation (i.e. praise), then you may be surprised when the feedback you receive is rather more than you bargained for.

Be clear about what you want feedback about and negotiate the scope of the conversation with the giver if necessary. Express your thoughts and feelings in a logical and concise manner.

Be transparent about why you want the feedback and *how* you think it can benefit both parties.

Be honest with yourself and the giver of the feedback. You may not hear what you want to hear; this may not feel so good. It's also possible that you may not feel able to change a situation or make improvement, so don't over-commit to change or improve until you have the support you need.

Plan. If you're looking for something more detailed than a quick indication that you're on the right track, don't spring your request on the other person. Arrange a meeting and prepare beforehand – in the same way as you would if you were planning to give feedback. Think about how you might want to move forward after the feedback. You might want to ask for coaching, mentoring or other support. It might be useful to ask the other person to be your 'accountability partner' by checking-in with you on your progress and improvement. By being dynamic about taking responsibility for your own professional development you will take charge of your own destiny; you will be seen as someone who is keen to improve and you won't be a victim of your own job history.

Think about how you have responded to feedback in the past. What thoughts and emotions did you experience in the lead-up to your feedback conversation? When you left the room how did you feel? How can you prepare and centre yourself so that you can make good use of the feedback you will receive?

The aim is for both parties to stay relaxed and able to focus on actively listening – and you can influence this even if you are the receiver not the giver. Being aware of emotions and managing the emotions in the room (which can include saying how you feel) means that both people are then free to engage with the learning points and messages and develop these into action points for future development.

Here are some suggestions for making the most of feedback you receive (as you can see, they are in line with best practice for *giving* feedback):

- ➢ Listen to it (rather than concentrating on preparing your response/defence)

- ➢ Ask for it to be repeated if you did not hear it clearly or if you want to check that you have understood correctly. Ask for examples

- ➢ Assume it is constructive until proven otherwise; then consider and use those elements that are constructive

- ➢ Pause and think before responding – if necessary, arrange another meeting rather than responding immediately

- ➢ Accept feedback positively (for consideration) rather than dismissively (for self-protection)

- ➢ Ask for suggestions of ways you might modify or change your behaviour

- ➢ Thank the person giving feedback

- ➢ Regard the feedback as though it was a gift of clothing. It may not fit you or you may decide to alter it or decide not to wear it at all

Dealing with inaccurate or badly given feedback

If you disagree with the feedback, both you and the giver can focus on finding points of agreement, so that you can specify and deal with the area of disagreement:

> ➢ Hear the person out and only then respectfully point out any inaccurate information

> ➢ Confirm the accurate parts of what is being said and agree with those

> ➢ Agree that an observation or point of view may be possible even if extremely unlikely

> ➢ Acknowledge the other person's logic even if you don't agree with what they say

Assume that the person giving you feedback does so with positive intention even though it may not resonate with you that way. They may be doing their best, but do not have the skills to give feedback in the most effective way. If this is the case, then you can help yourself to get the most out of the conversation by asking yourself these questions:

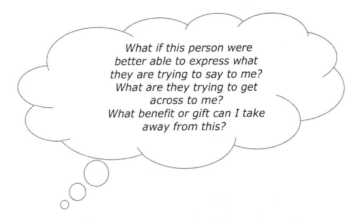

What if this person were better able to express what they are trying to say to me? What are they trying to get across to me? What benefit or gift can I take away from this?

Then you can see past or overlook your reaction and its unhelpful 'noise', leaving you free to get the most out of the conversation.

Conclusion

Remember that your aim is to help to create a culture of reflective practice where people can give and receive feedback honestly and fairly:

> ➤ Model what effective feedback looks like in both formal and informal conversations – ask for feedback yourself and receive it positively

> ➤ If necessary, request training, mentoring or coaching for yourself so that you can learn the skills you need to give, receive and ask for feedback as part of your career development

> ➤ Help your team members to make feedback part of the normal work-life of your team.

> ➤ Help team members to understand that feedback is an opportunity for learning and something to be valued and encouraged

> ➤ And most importantly, make time for feedback conversations – the investment will more than repay you and the team

Applying this to your workplace:

a) What lessons can you take away and use from the brief exchange between Blair and his manager Casey?

b) Reflect on your own experiences of giving/receiving feedback. Is there anything you would like to do differently now?

c) Have you been putting off a feedback conversation? What are the risks – to you, to your colleagues, to your team and your organisation of doing nothing? If you now feel ready to have that conversation, start planning your next steps

d) How can you get into the habit of asking for feedback on a regular basis?

Further references

➤ Stone, D. and Heen, S., *Thanks for the feedback – the science and art of receiving feedback well*, Penguin, 2015

➤ If you would like to read the article on feedforward and/or use the BROFF process, refer to www. learningcorporation.co.uk/Library

12

How come I'm doing what you could be doing? Delegating without resentment

Introduction

What does 'delegation' mean to you? Do you see delegation as a professional development opportunity or a source of irritation and frustration; the sign of a manager abdicating responsibility, or an indication of their trust and confidence in you and your skills? If you have management responsibilities – though perhaps without the official title – are you worried about handing over authority in this way because your intention might be misconstrued? Delegation – usually closely linked with prioritisation and decision-making – takes practice, so if you're not already in the habit, why not start now?

Here are some scenarios which are addressed in this chapter.

'I know I'm working extremely long hours and ought to delegate more. I think I know how to do it, so why do I keep talking myself out of it?'

'My manager thinks she's delegating work to me, but she's actually briefing me how to do work that's in my job description. She has bags of opportunity to delegate some of her own work. I'm not being developed in this organisation.'

'I dread Fridays. I can guarantee a manager will dump extra work on me, telling me it must be completed that day. They could give me at least a week's notice if they knew how to plan their time.'

'Julian always pushes back when I try and delegate work to him. He has the capability and the capacity and wants a salary increase! I wonder if he feels he would be taking on too much of a risk?'

We define delegation as 'giving someone the authority to do your own work or to act on your behalf, whilst ultimately retaining the responsibility for the successful completion of the task'. However, how we interpret the word delegation, and the process of delegating or being delegated to, depends very much on context, the people involved, the reasons for delegating, our situation and motivation at the time, and how the process is organised.

Effects of cultural contexts

Cultural contexts can impact on the practice of delegation. In some national cultures, additional responsibilities within organisations only go with a change of role and promotion. On the other hand, in Western Europe, for example, taking on delegated responsibility is usually part of the path to promotion – an opportunity to gain the experience and prove your competence *before* applying for the role.

Organisational culture also plays a significant role.

> Some large, more traditional hierarchical organisations tend to delegate major tasks through formal quarterly progress and objective-setting meetings, where individual performance against objectives is recorded. Being given short notice of delegated tasks tends to happen in project teams when team members can be asked to take on additional tasks for the sake of the team. These tend not to be recorded

> In small organisations it is more common for work to be delegated at short notice, as and when the work comes in. As the culture is informal, delegated tasks are not recorded and individual effort and contribution can easily be overlooked

> In high performing teams an indicator of their high level of collaborative working is noticing that individual team members see the work that needs to be done, step forward and take on the tasks themselves without being asked and with a blurring of individual role responsibilities

Everyone needs to know how to delegate

Of course, delegation isn't the sole prerogative of the leader or manager. As team-working is becoming more complex, team members need to be more adaptable and increasingly multi-skilled. The smooth running of the team also requires that team members, as well as team leaders, know which qualities and competencies colleagues can offer and how to pull on those qualities and competencies when needed. It's never too soon to start finding out more about the qualities and competencies of colleagues and getting clarity on the shared purpose of the team.

You also saw in the tasks/relationship model in Chapter 1 that as people progress in an organisation, they are likely to need to spend more of their time on relationships and less time doing tasks. They discover that the main way to reallocate their overall time is through practising the art of delegation – a skill we suggest you learn to master as soon as you have more junior people working with you.

In day-to-day situations you may find yourself taking the lead with juniors to support, simply because you're the only one available at that time. In this chapter we'll be looking at stages of the delegation process and how effective delegation can support good working relationships, boost motivation, make a genuine contribution to individual professional development and enhance team performance.

Barriers to delegation

Why don't people delegate? Often coaching clients shudder at the prospect. Relating back to the three basic drivers in Chapter 9, here are some of their valid reasons. Do any of the following sound familiar to you?

Driver A

➢ I love doing the work myself – that's what motivates me

➢ Other people won't do it as well as I can

➢ Others don't have my skills/expertise to do it well

➢ It will get done – but not in the way I would like it to be done

Driver B

➢ I fear that colleagues may not like me if I give them more work

> ➤ I worry about possible unpleasantness if I need to follow-up on work not done

Driver C

> ➤ I need to be seen/noticed by... so it's important that I'm seen to be part of the success

> ➤ I enjoy meeting external decision-makers and influencers

> ➤ I might lose status in the organisation if this person does the job well, or becomes the main client contact

General reason

> ➤ I don't have the time to explain the task – it's easier and quicker if I get on with it myself

Certain sectors of industry may have other reasons – for example, a law firm may have a performance management system that rewards lawyers based on the fees they personally bill to clients. Therefore, individual lawyers try to maximise their own time charged to the clients. An unfortunate consequence of this system is that their team members become under-utilised, de-motivated and better staff leave the organisation.

The delegation process: planning what to delegate

The feeling of being 'put upon' often arises when the task has been delegated 'out of the blue' with no advance notice or preparation. So, for maximum effectiveness, plan ahead, and think about which tasks recur every year, or every month. Plan your own time and responsibilities, ideally on a weekly basis. Also think about the tasks that are likely to need to be done over the next 2–4 weeks to help you to identify tasks which could be delegated.

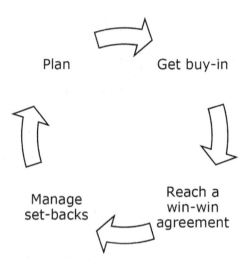

Plan   Get buy-in

Manage set-backs   Reach a win-win agreement

Having spent some personal time preparing what to delegate, decide to whom you want to delegate and the potential 'win' for that person. Then have a face-to-face and two-way discussion with the person who you would like to do the work.

Please see the links at the end of this chapter for further guidance on selecting the tasks that could be delegated, a form to plan the tasks to delegate and some tips on creating well-formed outcomes.

Manage setbacks

What if the task isn't well done – or not done at all?

You will try to avoid this happening by knowing the skills and strengths of the person you have chosen for the task, and by agreeing at the outset what 'excellence' looks like. However, if things do go wrong, here are three temptations that you need to resist:

> deciding not to delegate to that person again

> micro-managing them while they do the task – 'to make sure they get it right this time'

> taking over the task yourself.

Any of these responses may be a quick short-term fix – for you or for them – but long term will only serve to decrease trust, confidence and motivation. Think again about how you set up the task in the first place – what additional support might this person need (encouragement to write down what has been agreed, the opportunity to check in with you or another colleague to make sure they are on the right track, upskilling?) – then talk through what has gone wrong so that you can establish a new way of working in the future. For guidance on giving feedback see Chapter 11.

Think about what you know of this colleague:

> Are they the sort of person who typically says 'yes' to taking on additional tasks and responsibilities? If so, are they taking on too much?

> Are you delegating fairly? Are you relying too much on this colleague because they are keen and usually say 'yes'? As a result, maybe other colleagues are not getting the upskilling opportunities they need

> Do they feel they really have the option to say 'no' to you, or to themselves?

This colleague may be very willing to pull their weight in the team, and keen to learn. If you offer self-motivating colleagues like this a genuine opportunity to say that they can't take on this task, many will bounce back with renewed determination and enthusiasm. However, this doesn't necessarily mean that they will be able to get it done in the way you need, and in the timeframe required. In this case, go back to carefully talking through the why, what, how, when, etc. with the aim of reaching a shared understanding of what a successfully completed task looks like.

What about the reluctant delegatee?

Managing expectations is important here. Routine work happens at every level of an organisation and it's not possible for everyone to 'cherry-pick' the tasks they consider to be most interesting or worthwhile. Nevertheless, so-called 'routine tasks' are also important – a poorly photocopied set of documents says something about the lack of professionalism of the person who did them – and gives a poor overall impression of the team or organisation. Make sure that when delegating tasks, you explain (a) how the completed task will fit into the bigger picture, e.g. 'This is appendix A of the report we are sending to the client on Thursday afternoon'; and (b) why it is important to get it right first time.

Follow-up by expressing appreciation when the job is well done, mentioning the specific features that pleased you.

What do you do about the person who clearly does not want to take on the task even though you have given them ample notice?

Here are some tips:

> Listen carefully to the person's reasons, check that you have understood them correctly and

then provide any additional information and reassurances

➤ Depending on the task it may be appropriate to tell the person that completing the task well will help indicate that they are ready for promotion (but make sure you are being genuine rather than manipulative)

➤ If you have a good idea of what motivates the person, appeal to their main driver(s), e.g.

> ➤ Driver A: 'This is a challenging/new task and an opportunity to show our manager your capabilities'
>
> ➤ Driver B: 'By completing this task you will really help me/the team'
>
> ➤ Driver C: 'This task will give you an opportunity to meet X or to represent our department'

➤ If they seem to be a 'big picture person' you could explain how the task fits into the organisation's mission or vision or into a much larger initiative. If they are more of a 'details person' you could offer to break the task to be delegated into smaller packages and explain the task step by step

➤ The Theorist in the team may need more background information. The Pragmatist may need to be persuaded of the value of this completed task to the client or the organisation. (You may want to check Chapter 3 for a reminder about these different preferences)

➤ You could relate the task to the person's job role and remind them that this task is part of their job description

> ➤ If all else fails then it might be appropriate for you or your manager to give some feedback to this reluctant debutant, using the guidance in Chapter 11

Is there a case for not delegating?

There will be instances when it is not appropriate to delegate a task, either at all, or to certain staff members. Some examples are when:

> ➤ There is such a tight deadline that you need to complete the work yourself

> ➤ The task you are thinking of delegating would result in the delegatee seeing confidential information that your manager does not want other people to see

> ➤ The potential delegatee is leaving the team soon and it would be wrong to introduce this person to the client, particularly when staff continuity is important to the client

> ➤ The colleague does not have the skills/competencies/experience to carry out the task effectively – or the time to be trained

> ➤ A new, exciting piece of work has just come in and you are 80% through a complicated task. It is better for you to complete the remaining 20% and delegate the new piece of work

The benefits of planned delegation – the 'why' of delegation

Delegation to you, the delegator, enables you to:	*Delegation to you, the 'delegatee', enables you to:*	*Over time the organisation, clients, customers, stakeholders and partners notice:*
Reduce your workload	Experience new types of work and/or new clients	Higher staff retention
Improve your work-life balance	Enjoy more challenge and variety	More talented staff
Re-prioritise your time	Get to know your manager	Easier succession planning
Help develop staff	Demonstrate your readiness for promotion	Greater personal links between your staff and client's staff
Keep staff motivated, stretched, happy	Meet new people	Stronger client relationships
Take on new and/or more challenging work	Work at new locations	Distributed leadership, collaborative working and a coaching culture
Demonstrate collaborative leadership style	Make a favourable impression	Accelerated staff development
Increase your network/influence with staff	Feel you are making a greater contribution and can be trusted	Reduction in the composite charge-out rate to clients
Still 'be seen' to be in charge		Reduction in bottlenecks, overload, burn-out among senior staff
Share out successes		
Build a successful team		

Relax more on holiday	See work through a wider lens	Senior staff now spending more
Have more time to lead	Enhance your understanding of professionalism	time on strategic thinking, business development and specialist services
Enjoy more time to think strategically	Learn to take greater personal responsibility	
Build your coaching/ mentoring skills	Work more autonomously	
	Learn to juggle your time more effectively	
	Work with other technical disciplines	

Conclusion

With so many advantages, it's surprising that delegation is so often poorly attempted or indeed avoided altogether! We hope that this chapter has given you the confidence and the tools to enhance your delegation skills. Practising these skills will help you to make the best use of your time, allowing you to focus on those tasks that require your experience and expertise. It will also strengthen team-working and provide colleagues with valuable personal and professional development opportunities.

We have focused on delegating work to more junior team members. You can also delegate sideways and ask your peers to help out. If you have good rapport with more senior members of staff and you are skilled in the art of flattery you can also delegate upwards!

People are motivated by interesting work, job satisfaction, challenge, increasing responsibility and recognition[1] – intrinsic factors which answer people's deep-seated need for growth, personal development and achievement (for more on motivation at work see Chapter 9). Effective delegation has a pivotal role to play in increasing employee motivation and thereby enhancing team performance. Furthermore, in today's changeable, high-pressured and often stressful work environments, skilled and intentional delegation also supports sustainable working by protecting the long-term health and well-being of individual team members and the whole team.

Applying this to your workplace

a) Reflecting on your own experience and reactions, think about a specific instance when being delegated to was satisfying, rewarding and motivating. What made it so?

b) Having read this chapter, what changes would you like to make to the way you

   ➢ delegate work?

   ➢ motivate yourself and others?

c) Refer to 'Selecting the topics to be delegated and conducting the delegation conversation' by logging onto www.learningcorporation.co.uk/Library

---

[1] Frederick Herzberg, *Motivation to work*, Transaction Publishers, 1993.

Further references

- Cooper, Clay M., *Delegation: the key to leadership*, CreateSpace Independent Publishing Platform, 2015

- Stitt, Dave, *Deep and deliberate delegation: a new art for unleashing talent and winning back time*, 21CPL Productions, 2018

- Wenger, Shelley, *Delegation bundle*, CreateSpace Independent Publishing Platform, 2018

Part three

Succeeding in special circumstances

13

Is there anybody out there? Working in a dispersed or virtual team

Introduction

Virtual or dispersed workplaces have become a common phenomenon and they can take many forms. Do any of the following situations apply to you? If 'yes', this chapter is for you.

Example	Applies to me (tick)
I work from home one or more days in the week.	
I work 100% from home and only occasionally go into one of our offices.	
I am, or will be, seconded to a client for many months.	
We all work in different locations either in the same country or in different countries, perhaps in different time zones.	

I work in a matrix environment. (By 'matrix' we mean, for example, you might be based in Hamburg and your line manager is based in Frankfurt. For 20% of your time you work in a virtual project team and your project manager is based in Bangalore.)	
I work in a virtual or dispersed team and feel disconnected with my friends at work and with my organisation.	

Parts of this chapter are in note form as we wish to share many practical tips with you, whilst keeping the chapter brief.

Benefits of virtual teams

Virtual teams can be an attractive proposition to organisations for several reasons, particularly in industry sectors where talented staff are scarce. For example, they:

➤ enable the organisation to tap into a wider geographical talent pool

➤ help retain good employees, especially those who need to be more home-based, for example to take care of an elderly parent

➤ increase the diversity pool if potential specialist recruits live in other countries

➤ are an attractive recruitment strategy for people who would otherwise be turned off joining the organisation because of the time and cost spent commuting to and from work

➢ enable employees to work more flexible hours, achieve a better work-life balance and concentrate on their work in a more peaceful setting

➢ enable some service businesses to continue operating during national strikes or pandemics

➢ are essential for organisations which need to function 24 hours a day. They achieve this by having, for example, some staff based in Europe and other staff located in an entirely different time zone, say in the Asia Pacific

➢ help organisations to rationalise office space and its associated costs

Being a member of a virtual team can create challenges, for example:

➢ team members feeling lonely, 'distant' or left out, forgotten, or cut off from regular social interactions with team members; this disconnection may result in lower productivity and/or staff leaving the organisation

➢ team members failing to realise that they need to communicate with each other more frequently than in a traditional team where members sit near each other in the same building

➢ feeling that you're being pulled in different directions by being accountable to two or more 'bosses'

➢ being required to take part in frequent conference calls at unsocial hours

➢ finding it difficult to trust other members of the team you have not met before and/or where you have no experience of their personal trustworthiness or the quality of their work

➢ having a manager who hasn't grasped that running a virtual team requires a different mind-set, new skills, behaviours and team processes

➢ difficulty in contacting a colleague when you need a quick decision

➢ being expected to read and answer emails in your personal time

➢ suffering from anxiety, stress and mental health problems for any of the above reasons

Setting up a virtual team for success

Preparing for the first meeting

If you are asked to join, or perhaps head up, a new virtual (project) team, we encourage you to have all members of the team physically present for the inaugural 'kick-off' meeting. (Here's an opportunity to apply the influencing skills we shared with you in Chapter 8.)

The above challenges of virtual working should help you build the case for a residential kick-off meeting. Most of the meeting time should be spent getting to know each other, building rapport and trust and finding out each person's expectations and concerns about being a member of this team.

The topics to be covered should include:

➢ why the team is being created and how the team's work is aligned with the organisation's overall mission, vision and business strategies

➢ what the team is being asked to achieve; this should involve creating a shared vision of what this highly successful, completed project will look like, including clear, measurable outcomes

➢ why each person has been selected and the roles of each person

➢ some activities to help team members get to know each other to build rapport and trust and share their preferred working styles

➢ how you are going to work together including agreeing your team's core values and behaviours, your communication and data-sharing processes and how the team will make decisions

➢ why frequent communication is key to the success of the team

After this initial face-to-face meeting, subsequent meetings are likely to be virtual with face-to-face meetings held as frequently as is practicable.

Agreeing a Team Plan

A tool which we find useful to complete at the team formation stage is a Team Plan, a copy of which is in Chapter 7.

This plan will take two or more meetings to complete. Managers should resist the strong temptation to complete it themselves, as team members are more likely to implement it if they have been properly involved from the outset.

The challenges of communication

With team members based in different locations, communicating effectively with each other is a challenge. Emails are a quick way to get tasks off your desk, but in many instances, they can be ineffective and potentially damaging.

How many times a week have you sent an email or text message and then worried :

> ➢ Has the recipient received my email?

> ➢ Have they read it properly?

> ➢ Did they understand what I was trying to say?

> ➢ How have they reacted to my email? (You can't see their body language.) Have I caused offence?

> ➢ Are they going to act on my email, or at least reply?

With phone calls you not only experience the words themselves but also the tone, pitch, volume and variation in the voice ('the music'). These give you more clues about your colleague's level of, e.g., agreement, enthusiasm, energy and concerns.

Using a communication and data-sharing platform

Being able to see the other person is even better. Virtual team-working will benefit from using new generations of technology where you are able to share data and see the colleagues you want to communicate with. With some systems you can 'call up' the documents that are being discussed in the meeting as well as being able to see your colleagues who are on the call.

Your organisation may already use a bespoke system or have implemented, e.g., Zoom, Slack, MS Teams, Skype or Google Hangout. However, some platforms can't be used in some countries. For example, currently we cannot use Skype when we are coaching executives based in countries such as Oman, the UAE or China.

In our view it is preferable to choose a communication and data-sharing platform with proven reliability and security rather than one which uses the latest cutting-edge technology.

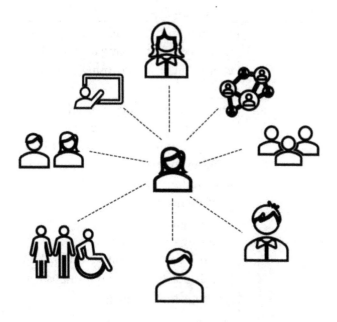

Communicating in a dispersed/virtual team

Setting up successful communications

The first thing to agree is how you are going to communicate with each other. We encourage you to develop a protocol covering:

Topic	Ideas to include in protocol
Choice of communication method	List types of communications, e.g. email, phone, video call, face-to-face meeting, with examples of when it is appropriate to use each type

Good practice re video calls	State your name each time you speak if one or more listeners cannot see you on their screens
	Listen attentively and let people finish what they want to say without talking over them or interrupting them in other ways
Frequency and timing of calls	Agree the frequency of whole-team conference calls, varying the starting time if team members are working in different time zones so that the same person does not always have to get up at 03.00 hours!
Cultural considerations	Some team members may appreciate receiving documents to read in advance of calls because it suits their learning style, or because English is not their first language
	Use clear language. With global teams it is likely that English has been adopted as the business language. English native speakers need to remember to use plain language and speak clearly. Even when speaking to a colleague in another English-speaking country it is important to clarify what the other person means when they say things like 'first base' or even 'urgent', as a word or phrase often has a different meaning in different countries

Accessibility	Bear in mind that a team member may not be able to pick up emails or calls whilst working at a client's premises or at some remote location
Clarity when delegating	When delegating work to a colleague who is working remotely, to avoid misunderstandings, ask them to confirm in writing the steps they propose to take to complete the task. Review and agree this before the work commences
Format of notes of meetings/ phone calls	The rest of the team will want to be updated when only a few members of the team are on a call to discuss a specific issue, or a single member of the team has a conversation with a client. Summarise the conversation and provide a link to the full notes of the meeting on the organisation's intranet

Encouraging successful virtual relationships

Developing trust and recognising diversity

You need to compensate for the fact that team members will not benefit from casual conversations in the office corridor or at the water fountain or over lunch. When you 'meet' virtually:

> Build in time for social chit chat, especially so if some members have never met face to face. Those team members who are 'people persons' will immediately

see the necessity of this, whilst those who are more task-focused may need to learn the importance of 'small talk' and patience

➤ If some team members believe that it is more difficult to maintain concentration when engaged in virtual meetings one obvious remedy is to keep the business part of meetings focused and brief

➤ Have regular feedback sessions (Chapter 11) to discuss how things are going, not only about the tasks but also about the quality of interpersonal relationships

Managing conflict

When any group of people work together, they may develop the habit of complaining about each other, either in meetings or off-line. This can often happen because of cultural differences – for example how different cultures construe what 'being on time' means or because of different working styles. Alternatively, there is the danger that members may shy away from disagreeing with each other for fear of upsetting a colleague. 'Group think' can then set in, which may result in poor decision-making. As this danger may be more prominent in virtual team-working it is important to find ways to encourage team members to 'speak up' and express their opinions.

Should there be signs that conflict is growing between some members, many practical tips on avoiding and resolving conflict are given in Chapter 14.

Protecting intellectual property (IP) including copyright

It is more difficult to protect copyright and other forms of intellectual property in a virtual environment compared to a traditional team. For example, a team member might be seconded to a client and become involved in jointly developing with the client a product or a system or service. It is quite likely that the team member will draw on the experience gained in your own company and inadvertently share your company's copyright material or other valuable IP. At the end of this project your company is left with the problem of who owns the IP in this jointly developed product, system or service.

Therefore, with staff secondments to external clients, managers need to make sure there is a clear and comprehensive protocol regarding IP and the use of other confidential information, and that there is a written agreement with the client.

Maintaining momentum

> Coming together is a beginning; keeping together is progress; working together is success.
>
> (Henry Ford)

As with other types of teams there is usually a lot of enthusiasm and goodwill during the formation stage. Due to the special challenges of being in a virtual team, the risk of losing momentum is higher than in a traditional team. For example, the manager, being based at a different location, will find it more difficult to check on progress and quality of work. And it's not just about monitoring and control – the manager will not be available for the kinds of quick and informal conversations that face-to-face contact makes easy and which serve to maintain focus, encouragement, support and motivation.

Here are some practical tips to help maintain momentum:

Interim deadlines	Break down the main tasks and outcomes into small manageable packets of work and agree deadlines to complete each package Create a culture of shared ownership and leadership of the project by, for example, allocating certain tasks to small sub-groups or individuals to manage, with agreed deadlines (especially important in larger virtual teams)
Visual progress chart	Allocate tasks to team members and record them on a Gantt Chart so that all team members can see their own and each other's progress against the plan
Weekly check-ins	Have short, weekly check-ins where each person shares their progress, their concerns, their progress to date and their main tasks and challenges for the coming week
Early warnings	Be open about any problem at the earliest opportunity and share ideas on how to overcome it
Support each other	Recognise that in a matrix environment each person will have other responsibilities and seasonal pressures and therefore team members should be willing to work flexibly to share the work at peak times
Make it enjoyable	Increase the connection between individuals by trying to make virtual working as enjoyable as possible, e.g. spend part of regular team meetings on personal updates, social topics and include a social networking platform in the shared workspace

Keep in touch	Check on each person's well-being as well as their technical progress and challenges, and encourage all members to keep in touch with each other on a 1 to 1 basis. This will generally be initiated by the team manager, but all team members can be encouraged to maintain their relationships this way
Learn from the best	Read articles and books about virtual teams and talk to virtual teams in other industry sectors about how they have overcome the 'social distance' and achieve high performance

Conclusion

Virtual team-working is already widespread, and its use is likely to increase. The 'Office in your Pocket', together with other future advances in technology, will provide essential aids to team members but technology by itself is not the answer to the challenges of working virtually. Make human engagement the first priority. Building rapport, credibility and trust and communicating with attentive listening skills will still be paramount, supported by the many tips we have provided in this and other chapters.

Applying this to your workplace

a) What lessons have you learned from this and earlier chapters that could help to make your virtual team more effective? For example:

> ➢ to overcome the feeling of being cut off from the team

> ➤ to improve the quality of communications

> ➤ to guard against the loss of copyright?

b) How might you share the tips in this and other chapters with your team or your team leader?

Further references

> ➤ Hall, K., *Making the matrix work: how matrix managers engage people and cut through complexity,* Nicholas Brealey International, 2013

> ➤ *Leading virtual teams,* HBR 20-Minute Manager Series, Harvard Business School Press, 2016

> ➤ Shawbell, D., *Back to human: how great leaders create connections in an age of isolation,* Piatkus, 2018

14

Ouch! That wasn't nice! Handling challenging relationships

Introduction

Have you ever found yourself in one of these challenging relationships, or something like it?

> *'Every time I [Mike] go to pick up the phone and see that it is Zhiyuan who is calling me, I turn into a quivering wreck.'*

> *'I don't get on well with my new line manager. He always seems to be preoccupied and snaps at me whenever I try to talk to him, so now I just keep a low profile and stay out of his way.'*

> *'It infuriates me that x always gets her way at management meetings. We all seem to fall for her emotional blackmail, and no one seems to know how to stop it.'*

> *'Well, there's being direct and there's being downright rude! Where did that comment come from?'*

Which kind of relationships do you find most challenging at work – people who are angry, people who show their emotions, people who move too fast, or too slow, people who talk too much, or too little…?

Pause for reflection…

Think about people you find challenging at work… for whatever reason. Keep them in mind as you work through this chapter…

What happens to you when you're on the receiving end of a rude comment or direct feedback from an overly critical colleague? Relationships that you perceive as challenging can lower your energy levels, spoil your enjoyment at work and affect your general well-being.

When faced with an unsatisfactory relationship at work or at home, you may be prompted to wonder whether the problematic relationship is due to lack of rapport and trust, or a breakdown in communication. Perhaps you were communicating on different wavelengths or something you said impacted on the other person in a way you hadn't anticipated? It is possible also that an unhelpful – though secretly held – mind-set about the other person has somehow 'leaked' into the relationship. Alternatively, an imbalance of power within the relationship may be undermining easy communication.

This chapter gives you many practical tips on how to improve relationships with people that you find challenging, so that you can get back on track to enjoying your work and building effective relationships.

We could have written a whole book on handling challenging people situations – indeed, potentially we have! The basics in our foundation chapters (1–6) are the absolute cornerstones that will help you manage challenging relationships. The tips we shared with you in previous chapters, such as those about having excellent listening skills and giving feedback properly, will also help you deal with challenging people situations.

Managing challenging relationships needs to be considered in four phases:

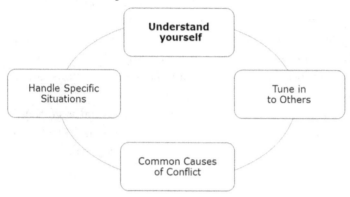

Understand yourself

One of the most intriguing and challenging quotations we know is: *'The distance between yourself and another person is the same as the distance between yourself and yourself'* (Richard Moss).

Taking personal responsibility

Imagine that you are complaining to another person about one of your colleagues. Your arm is outstretched with a finger pointing towards the person who is causing you problems. Now notice that whilst one finger is pointing away from you, three of your fingers are pointing back towards you. It is as though these three fingers are telling you that it is your responsibility to improve the relationship. You can't assume that you can change the other person. The only person you can change is yourself. This gives you the responsibility, but it also gives you the power, to take action to improve things.

Stimulus and response

Let's go back to what Mike said at the beginning of this chapter. Zhiyuan is phoning (stimulus) and Mike reacts (response) immediately and automatically, almost like a robot. What if Mike could, instead, put a gap (in this case 5+ seconds) between the stimulus and his response? This would give him time to choose how he wants to respond; time to choose his emotional state as well as his words. As mentioned in Chapter 4, in any given situation Mike has more than two options for how he can respond. How many options can you think of in Mike's situation? Five? Ten?

If you are in a difficult relationship, what is getting in the way? Perhaps it is a habitual reactive behaviour they set up in you, particularly on a bad day. Is it for example:

➤ pride

➤ jealousy

➤ desire for power or control

➤ fear

➤ anger

➤ other?

Pause for reflection...

Consider one of your challenging relationships. Which of the emotions listed above (or it might be a different emotion) has an influence on how you respond to your colleague? Be curious; don't judge yourself – just be intrigued to notice what happens when you interact with them...

Reconsidering your mind-set

As we mentioned in Chapter 4, one of the ways we are unique is in the way we have created our own library of mind-sets, learned and consolidated over time, which influence how we think about our own capabilities, our manager, market competition and that 'difficult person'. Most of our mind-sets are up to date and effective. However, one or two mind-sets may be incomplete, or out of date, or totally incorrect.

If Mike continues to operate out of the same mind-set about Zhiyuan and keeps to the same behaviour, i.e. becomes a quivering wreck, he will continue to get what he's always got, that is to feel he is being treated like a doormat. One of the actions Mike can take is to reconsider his mind-set about Zhiyuan.

Pause for reflection...

How would you describe your mind-set about a 'difficult person' you work with?

What experiments could you make to change your mind-set and behaviour until you notice a positive shift in the other person's behaviour?

In Chapter 6 we talked about the importance of listening to a colleague in order to establish a connection with them. One of the best experiments you could make in your challenging relationship would be the simple act of giving them your undivided attention and the space for them to be heard. As Gandhi said, *'The greatest need of the human soul is to be understood.'* Your attentiveness may calm the situation so that no further action is necessary. You will also find that the more you listen to a colleague, the more sense they make.

Here are some ideas from NLP (the study and modelling of excellence) which can help you change your mind-set about the person you find challenging:

➢ Change your perspective of the 'difficult person' by visualising them in less threatening ways. For example, imagine that you are watching this 'challenging person' on a television screen and that your magic remote control allows you to change the person's voice to make it quieter or to an amusing squeaky voice. You can change the picture to a dim black and white and you could continue to use your imagination by making the person much smaller and shrinking the picture so that it just occupies a small (harmless) postage stamp-sized area in the bottom right-hand corner of your screen

➢ Alternatively, you can visualise this person as a cuddly koala or a kitten. When you next meet this 'difficult person' you can take your new image of them into the meeting with you. Although the person is still the same, you will see and hear them as less intimidating and so be able to manage your emotions more effectively

➢ One of the most powerful NLP techniques that can help you find other possible options for dealing with the situation is a floor exercise called 'Perceptual Positioning'. This is a form of modelling that allows you to step into somebody else's shoes, and see what they see, hear what they hear, and feel what they feel. At the end of this chapter there is a link to how you can obtain a full explanation of this tool

Be attentive to how you communicate

How do you like people to communicate to you? In the rush for efficiency, it can be easy to miscommunicate. Even saying nothing at all is sending some sort of message – a space within which others are free to interpret a message, whether that message is correctly interpreted or not. For example, a colleague who walks past you in the corridor without acknowledging you, or looks uninterested when they are speaking to you and others at a meeting, risks conveying messages which will impact on your relationship.

Pause for reflection...

Think of a situation where someone annoyed or hurt you when they gave you a piece of feedback. Reflect on what happened and ask yourself, if your colleague had better interpersonal skills, how might they have spoken or written to you in a way that was acceptable to you?

Now turn it round and think about how the way in which you communicate may be interpreted by others. Perhaps you dashed off an email to which the recipient took offence; this may indicate that they have not understood what you were saying, or simply that they are getting sick of receiving emails from you when you could so easily speak to them face to face... How can you find out?

First aid for challenging situations

All of us can get nervous in some situations. You might like to use some of these techniques from NLP to help you be more grounded before you meet a 'difficult person' or approach a situation which could be stressful such as when you are about to give a presentation:

> ➤ Model your behaviour on someone you admire. Ask yourself, 'Who gets on well with this person? How do they behave?' or 'What would one of my heroes or heroines do in this situation?' Then you can select and adopt a specific piece of your hero's behaviour to use yourself

➢ Practise Positive Emotional Anchoring. This technique helps to ensure that your emotional state works for you and not against you when you are with, or about to meet, this 'difficult person'. For a detailed explanation of this process you could refer to www.nlpu.com/ encyclopedia under the heading 'anchoring'

A Master NLP Practitioner should be able to teach you Positive Emotional Anchoring, or how to create an imaginary protective shield or 'second skin', to help you create a resourceful mind-set when you would otherwise feel you are under attack.

Remember that every situation is an opportunity for learning and professional development.

Pause for reflection...

Looking at the above tips, which one(s) could help you with a relationship you would like to improve?

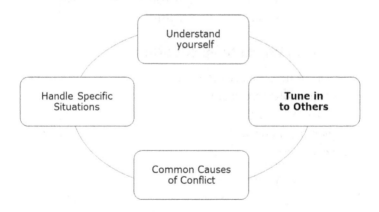

Understand yourself

Handle Specific Situations

Tune in to Others

Common Causes of Conflict

Tune in to others

Once you have considered the tips above to help you feel more resourceful, you can spend time tuning in to the way the other person likes to operate. The more you can think about how the other person views the situation/topic, the more successful your conversation will be:

> What do you know about how you prefer to communicate, and more importantly, how they prefer to communicate? For example, you may prefer to use visual and big picture language to express your ideas and feelings. But you have noticed that the other person prefers a combination of tangible kinesthetic words such as 'concrete examples', 'grounding' or 'getting a grip', together with detailed step-by-step arguments. Switch to their wavelength by using words and phrases like their preferred words and phrases

> Be prepared to shift the level of the conversation in order to meet your colleague on common ground. If the other person is referring to the organisation's mission, vision and values, this is 'high level' stuff. You may need to 'chunk up' and converse at their level before you introduce your topic. Alternatively, if the other person is talking in detail about such things as skills, behaviours, equipment or money, you may need to 'chunk down'. So, be aware of where *you* prefer to talk, put that to one side, find the common ground and first meet your colleague there

> Think hard about whether you may have made any incorrect assumptions about the other person or the situation. If you suspect that this might be the case, spend time determining the facts. Or they may be making a *generalisation,* in which case ask them for one or two specific instances so that you can be sure what they are talking about

Fix the problem, not the blame.

(Japanese proverb)

First aid for challenging meetings

Always separate the other person from the problem. Then put the problem 'out there' and work together to find a solution.

> ➤ Focus on the needs of the task rather than the other person. Ask the other person, 'What does the task or client want from us right now?'

> ➤ Be empathic towards the other person. You just don't know what is happening in their life. Bad behaviour is often a symptom of a deeper wound

> ➤ Ask the other person, 'How do you feel our business relationship is working?' If appropriate, then add, 'What could we do to make it (even) better?'

> ➤ If the person continues to irritate you, resist rising to the bait and continue to be respectful and courteous, remembering to focus instead on the work that needs to be done

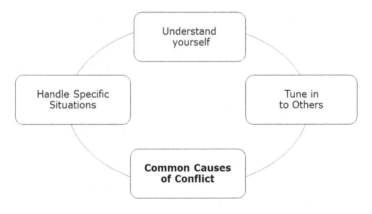

Other common causes of conflict

If you are in or on the edge of conflict with another person, it helps to understand what is likely to be the cause so that you can work on the cause and either avoid the conflict or minimise it. Although the following list is not exhaustive, in our experience the source of conflict is likely to be one of the following:

> Different values

> > One of your personal values may conflict with the other person's values. For example, 'fairness' may be one of your key values, but this may seem to be of trivial importance to the other person

> Divergent expectations

> > over quality, status, work distribution or deadlines

> Decision-making

> > Instances which could result in conflict might be when a decision has been made and a colleague who is directly affected by the decision says they were not consulted or that they felt rushed into deciding

> Assumptions

> > for example, about responsibilities, promises and commitments, e.g. 'I thought you were going to contact the client and you failed to do so'

> Different strong preferences

> > As we saw in Chapter 3, people have different preferences which come to the surface at work.

For example, one person may be a task-focused activist whilst the other person may be highly reflective and people-focused. Or one person may have a strong need for more data before making decisions and the other person may be highly intuitive and comfortable with less data

➤ Knowledge and expertise

➤ for example, about competence or the willingness to delegate, or where a colleague is too proud to admit that they did not know how to carry out a task and made a complete mess of it

➤ Goals

➤ Conflict may result from goals that are inappropriate, not clearly expressed or which keep changing. Perhaps you and your colleague are working to different agendas and different goals

➤ Roles

➤ A common problem is a lack of clarity over who does what, or one person starts to tread on another person's toes or is given work which should be given to a more junior person

➤ An over-used strength

➤ As we mentioned in Chapter 10, an over-used strength can damage relationships. For example, an over-used strength of self-assurance may come across as arrogance

➤ Pressures

➤ Some people thrive on pressure, others have a much lower threshold. Being under persistent pressure can be the underlying cause of tiredness, stress, irritability, short temper, making mistakes, all resulting in conflict

➤ The 'Storming phase'

    ➤ According to Bruce Tuckman,[1] a group or a team (or a committee) go through five distinct phases. Briefly the second stage is 'Storming'. Your team may have been created some time ago and yet the conflict in the team may be a sign that the team is still in the Storming phase or has fallen back into this phase. The causes of disquiet, frustration and conflict may be that expectations are not being met, roles are unclear, a feeling that a colleague is not an important or useful part of the team, or work has not been distributed evenly, or a new member has joined the team and is questioning some important decisions that were made prior to their arrival

First aid for common causes of conflict

Most of the points above can be addressed by bringing them into the open during initial planning meetings and discussing them. This takes extra time when you're probably keen just to get on with the job, but it prevents all sorts of problems later. The meanings of key terms, core values, roles and expectations can all be clarified up front – then when difficulties arise (and they will) you can come back to what you agreed, rather than being angry with each other.

If you are in the middle of a project and these conflicts have already occurred, rather than just trying to resolve

---

[1] Donald Egolf, *Forming storming norming performing: successful communication in groups and teams*, 3rd edition, iUniverse, 2013.

them one by one, propose that you have a time-out to create a working agreement for a good relationship.

Remember that some conflict can be creative and beneficial to the organisation. Conflict as disagreement over ideas or processes can be positive, especially when there is trust between the parties. Then they can both break free of binary (either/or) thinking in favour of implications thinking and start generating third or fourth or more alternative ways forward (as we covered in Chapter 4).

Pause for reflection...

Are you aware of conflict in your team? If so, which of the above are likely to be the cause of the situation – and how could you move forward to improve the working relationships within the team?

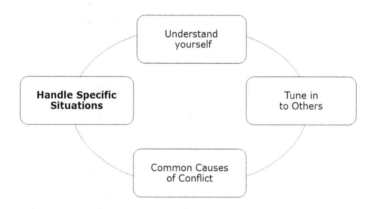

Handle specific situations

Here are two situations that are mentioned frequently in our workshops and coaching conversations – working with:

➢ a difficult manager

➢ an under-performing colleague

Here are some tips to supplement the tips given earlier in this and in other chapters.

A difficult manager

➢ Endeavour to understand your manager by putting yourself in your manager's shoes. Ask yourself questions like: What is on my manager's mind? What keeps my manager awake at night? What goals and targets is my manager expected to achieve? What pressures is my manager under? What is it that motivates my manager?

➢ When you are with your manager, talk about topics that are directly relevant to their role (rather than yours), e.g. about strategy, performance management, business development, a news item about your industry sector, or about one of your clients

➢ When your manager gives you a task to carry out, check you know why the task is required and how it fits into your manager's bigger picture. If your manager likes detail, find out precisely what you need to do. Clarify what a successfully completed piece of work looks like by their criteria, not yours, so that your expectations are aligned with your manager's

➢ Agree a deadline that you know you can meet easily. This gives you a bit of room for contingencies and the opportunity to deliver the completed task slightly ahead of the deadline

➢ You may already know the old saying *'Don't come to me with a problem, come to me with a solution.'* So, if there is a problem don't just dump it on your manager; think through the problem carefully, discuss it with your manager, mention at least one suggested solution and offer to help resolve the problem

➢ Find out from your colleagues what makes your boss tick. If one of your colleagues has a good relationship with your boss, ask this colleague for tips on how you might improve your relationship

➢ If your manager has upset you and you want to give them some feedback, start with 'I' rather than 'you'. For example, 'I think what you said about me at the management meeting this morning was most unfair.' This way you are making clear the impact the manager's behaviour has had on you rather than saying 'You are unfair', which could be taken as a judgement on your manager's character and could damage your already unsatisfactory relationship

➢ Have you come across this mythical radio station WII-FM ('what's in it for me')? There will be occasions when you can build into your completed assignment a personal WII-FM for your manager, e.g. an acknowledgement of the contribution they have made or an opportunity for your manager to meet an important potential client

➢ Prepare carefully for meetings with your manager and from the moment you enter the room behave in a friendly, confident manner. As Phyllis Diller said, '*A smile is a curve that sets everything straight*'

An under-performing colleague

Whilst continuing under-performance is normally handled by your line manager, you may be expected to deal with the under-performer if they are working in your project team. Here are some tips:

- ➤ Catch the under-performance at an early stage before it infects the team's morale

- ➤ Try and understand the underlying cause. If the person is new to the organisation don't assume that it was a recruitment error. We remember a senior manager joining the firm and after a few weeks he was obviously struggling. Some people started to mutter that the firm had made a mistake recruiting this person. However, we had a chat with him and found out that he was suffering from migraines, not because he found the work stressful but, unknown to him, the neon light in his office was throwing a creamy yellow light onto his working papers which was giving him a sick headache. After a change of neon tube his performance improved dramatically

- ➤ If the employee was once a high performer, ask them what might have caused the slip in performance and agree a pathway back

- ➤ When delegating work, be especially careful to ensure you both reach a shared understanding of what an excellent completed piece of work looks like, that the deadline is fully understood as well as the implications of not completing this work properly and before the deadline

- ➤ Break down longer pieces of work into smaller manageable stages and review each part before your colleague begins the next stage

- ➤ Recognise and acknowledge the other person's improvements. Even though you may think these improvements are small they may be much bigger steps for the person who is trying to raise their game

➤ Discuss any continued under-performance with your manager. The worst-case scenario is that the individual may need to be managed out of the organisation so that the rest of the team's performance is not affected, and the individual concerned has a chance to flourish in another organisation. However, don't start with this option in mind as the only solution – you could end up losing a potentially valuable colleague

For tips on how to handle three other specific situations that can cause difficulty –

➤ an older colleague

➤ the team member who brings personal problems into work

➤ the emotional blackmailer

– see the link at the end of this chapter

Re-establishing a relationship

Here are some more general suggestions as to how to re-establish a relationship which has stalled:

➤ Suggest a relationship relaunch. Both of you could complete the 'Holding the Mirror' exercise (see the link at the end of Chapter 7). Then meet to share what you have both written and contract how you want to work together

➤ If the other person seems to be inaccessible to you, ask about the best time of day to contact them and how they like to be contacted, e.g. face to face or by phone

➢ Suggest that the two of you meet for coffee to get to know each other better

➢ Try and arrange to work together on a future project with the expectation that work brings people together

➢ If there is disharmony in parts of the team, consider mapping the quality of relationships between the members of your team. We refer to a Mapping the Quality of Relationships tool at the end of this chapter

➢ Finally, if all else fails, can you carry out your responsibilities without needing to work with this colleague?

Pause for reflection...

Which of the above tips could help you improve a relationship which is challenging you, or a relationship you would like to make even better?

Conclusion

A truly 'difficult person' is extremely rare – you will probably go through your entire working life without meeting someone with whom neither you nor your colleagues are able to establish a working relationship.

When you encounter situations involving 'difficult' people, it is too easy to fall into the trap of assuming that the other person is at fault. Instead, without judging yourself, first go back to basics to find what you might have done or not done which may have triggered the adverse reaction from your colleague.

In this chapter we have covered a wide range of topics about handling difficult situations and challenging relationships. Practising the suggestions in this chapter will help you to reduce stress, bring back the fun and enjoyment of work, increase your effectiveness as well as your general well-being, and improve the team's performance.

Applying this to your workplace

a) How do you normally respond to challenging people situations? What do you need to do to become more resilient/effective?

b) At the beginning of this chapter we invited you to think of colleagues you find challenging at work. Prepare a brief outline plan for each person

c) Consider using three valuable resources mentioned in this chapter:

> ➤ Perceptual Positioning

> ➤ Mapping the Quality of Relationships

> ➤ Further tips on handling specific difficult situations

d) Copies of which are at www.learningcorporation.co.uk/ Library

Further references

> ➤ Egolf, Donald, *Forming storming norming performing: successful communication in groups and teams*, 3rd edition, iUniverse, 2013

- Kahane, Adam, *Collaborating with the enemy: how to work with people you don't agree with or like or trust*, McGraw-Hill Education, 2017

- Paton, Bruce and Stone, David, *Difficult conversations: how to discuss what matters most*, Penguin, 2011

- Seligman, Martin, *Learned optimism*, Vintage Books, 1991

- Shatte, Andrew and Reivich, Karen, *The resilience factor*, Broadway Books, 2003

- Wesley, Doug, *Conflict resolution in the workplace*, CreateSpace Independent Publishing Platform, 2015

15

The riches of diversity

Anneliese Guérin-Le Tendre

Diversity: the art of thinking independently together.
(Malcolm Forbes)

Introduction

Your organisation probably already has procedures in place
to comply with legislation on diversity; however, in this
chapter we invite you to go beyond the legal requirements,
beyond political correctness, even beyond personal
sensitivity to race, ethnicity or gender, to celebrating what
we all have in common – our differences.

When we recognise and value our differences, we create
an environment in which everyone has the opportunity to
be seen and to be heard; in which everyone is able to fulfil
their potential by putting their specific gifts to work. In an
environment where diversity is truly honoured, the positive
impact – on motivation, morale, communication, teamwork and performance and creativity – is stunning.

In this brief overview of a huge topic, we'll focus on a few
key points applicable immediately to your work situation:

➢ what we mean by 'culture' and 'diversity'

➢ why valuing the complexity of cultural diversity is important in teams, organisations and communities

➢ how 'unconscious bias' can filter through into the way team members communicate, and undermine good relationships at work – and what you can do about it

➢ how to be intentional about how you and your team communicate in a way that is genuinely inclusive

The case for cultural diversity

A compelling business case can be made for honouring diversity. Companies in the top quartile for gender, racial and ethnic diversity are more likely to have financial returns above their national industry medians; organisations committed to diverse leadership are more successful; those that value diversity are better able to win top talent and so improve their customer orientation, employee satisfaction, and decision-making.[2]

The same is true in public sector organisations, such as healthcare, where research confirms that patient care is best when there is a positive culture of respect, dignity and trust among staff.[3] However if the only driving force for honouring diversity is economic gain, public image

---

[2] V. Hunt, D. Layton and S. Prince, *Diversity matters*, McKinsey Consulting, 2015.

[3] M. West and J. Dawson, *NHS staff management & health service quality*, Department of Health & Social Care, 2011.

or 'political correctness', any initiative, policy or values statement is likely to fail.[1]

Diversity begins at home

So, how do you manage the power of diversity in a team? Often you hear people talking about diversity as though it's something that concerns only other people, and yet the best place to start is by recognising our own diversity, that is, the ways in which we are all unique. Then we are in a better position to recognise difference in others.

First, a quick questionnaire:

1. How would you describe your own identity? (e.g. 'I'm a/an... who... and... and...')

2. In what ways do you appreciate diversity in your everyday life?

3. Are there values which are important to you that might not seem important to others? (e.g. 'I seem to be the only one who cares about...')

4. What are your particular qualities, strengths, values, experiences – in other words, what does it mean to be *you*?

5. How have your attitudes and beliefs been developed – who or what were your influences?

If you felt a bit stumped by some of these questions, that wouldn't be surprising – you're experiencing our human condition; our identities and how we value difference in others are developed at a very early age and we are largely

---

[1] F. Dobbin and A. Kaley, 'Why diversity programs fail', *Harvard Business Review*, July–August 2016.

unconscious of them. As we grow, we learn from our experiences and discover how best to survive and thrive in our particular environment; we pick up values and beliefs, some of which are within our awareness, and others not. Our unconscious values and beliefs become integrated into our world view, manifesting themselves in our ways of thinking, our responses to the outside world, and interactions with others; they shape our assumptions about how the world is – or how it ought to be, according to our own perspective!

What do we mean by 'culture'?

> Two people belong to the same culture [if] they interpret the world in roughly the same ways and can express their ideas, their thoughts and feelings about the world, in ways which will be understood by each other.
>
> (S. Hall)[2]

You have probably read similar definitions before – and perhaps you are aware that national cultures tend to regard certain universal aspects of life – time, work, individual achievement, relationships – very differently.

Maybe you've also heard of the 'culture onion' whose layers represent the various aspects of culture; the outermost, visible, indicators of culture, then the norms, the values, through to the core of the onion – those assumptions, attitudes and beliefs which are central to our ways of being.

Visible cultural differences are accessible to outsiders, and observed and talked about by both 'insiders' and 'outsiders' quite openly and easily. As they get to know a culture, people become more curious to know more about

---

[2] Stuart Hall, *Representation: cultural representations and signifying practices*, 2nd edition, Sage, 2013.

what lies beneath the peculiarities. Visitors to the UK often comment on the way that queuing seems to be a British 'norm' – a behaviour that insiders apparently share and agree as being desirable. A visitor might be curious as to why this particular norm is respected – and what values it seems to point to: in this case, fairness (including the valuing of people's time) and courtesy. Not adhering to cultural norms such as this can incite various reactions ranging from disapproving body language to audible outrage!

Take a step further into the 'culture onion' and you discover that at the 'core' of any culture are the most profound attitudes, assumptions and beliefs that underpin it. These are generally learned and shared outside conscious awareness and are often not explained or talked about between members of the same culture – unless they are challenged or breached in some way. So to return to our example, beneath the apparently insignificant act of queuing and the expectations of fairness and politeness, sit the weightier values of justice and equality. At this level, shared identity is usually so profoundly felt that questioning the validity of core beliefs – whether from outside the culture, or from within – can arouse very strong emotions.

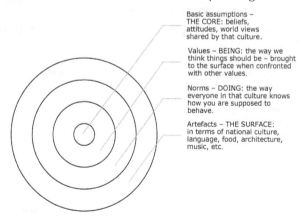

Basic assumptions –
THE CORE: beliefs,
attitudes, world views
shared by that culture.

Values – BEING: the way we
think things should be – brought
to the surface when confronted
with other values.

Norms – DOING: the way
everyone in that culture knows
how you are supposed to
behave.

Artefacts – THE SURFACE:
in terms of national culture,
language, food, architecture,
music, etc.

The culture onion

The complexity of cultural identity

Pause for a moment: do you identify yourself primarily with your home country, your region or your town – perhaps all of these? Maybe you also identify yourself with your family's country of origin. In the UK today, some people view themselves as citizens of the world or as Europeans, as much as British. Most of us integrate our past and present identities to greater or lesser extents, and in this way live with a depth and complexity of cultural richness.

While some aspects of our identity were fixed at birth or very early on, many are learned or adopted by choice, and expanded upon by our experience. People who share the same collective identity see themselves as having a common interest, purpose and view on the world. This is expressed in a rich store of values – for example, solidarity, justice, equality, democracy, freedom.

However, let's not limit our idea of culture to national norms, values and assumptions. The culture onion analogy can be applied to all cultural groups. As you begin to look at people through the lens of their complex cultural identity, their norms of behaviour, the values they hold dear and the core assumptions that drive them will emerge – and that is both interesting and helpful in building positive connections with others.

Influences of individual cultural identity

Culture and communication

In Chapter 5 we talked about communication, the process by which we 'make meaning' in order to understand each other. We said that we typically do that by creating a 'code book' of shared sociolinguistic rules which consciously or unconsciously govern our communication with each other. Culture is part of that 'code book' – the culture of home and family, friends and social groups, organisations, regions, or nations... If you work with team members who are based abroad, you might have stumbled over cultural attitudes towards aspects such as status and authority, risk-taking, information-sharing, and so on. Different perspectives on cultural assumptions like these can be puzzling, even frustrating, but once you become aware that you are playing by different 'rules', you can start to create your own, new, shared code book.

Cultural norms, values and assumptions provide 'context', so will of course impact on verbal and non-verbal communication. You will need to know about the cultural context of your colleagues and clients from other cultures, e.g. their understanding of words like *meeting, deadline, urgent, manager, lunch*. Although a more standardised 'global' English is spread by the media, business and the internet, in reality the use of English does not cancel out the impact of culture – cultural context changes understanding.

At the same time, while national preferences may be 'typical', individuals do not always conform to their national cultures any more than individuals always comply with family, generational, gender or team cultures, so tread lightly with generalisations: not all Germans are precise about time; not all Americans are wild extraverts; not all British people demonstrate emotional control! It is simplistic thinking about difference that creates division and breaks down trust – in teams, organisations, regions – and finally between countries. So, rather than resorting to stereotypes, be curious, share experiences, talk about the cultural norms of the countries represented in your team, listen and observe:

- ➤ How direct or indirect is their communication?
- ➤ What is the relative importance of verbal vs. non-verbal communication?
- ➤ How much formality or informality is expected?
- ➤ How easy is it to say 'no' in some cultures?
- ➤ Is brevity valued in communication?

Your own observations will reveal how cultural identity is highly individual, made up of the layers of influence from the many cultural groups to which we have belonged. In this sense all interpersonal communication can also be called 'intercultural'.

Difference, prejudice, and unconscious bias

Let's take a closer look at those other distinctions we sometimes make – consciously or unconsciously – which can separate us from other people. When you think about difference and diversity, what comes first to mind?

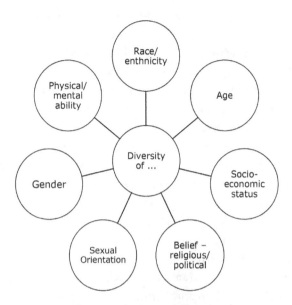

Seven main areas of diversity

We routinely and rapidly sort ourselves and others into categories – in our early history this capacity for categorisation acted as a protection, a 'danger indicator' which helped us to decide whether the other person or group represented a threat to our survival. The legacy of this biological hard-wiring is that we tend to prefer people who look like us, sound like us and share our interests; social psychologists call this phenomenon 'social categorisation'. Operating at a very subtle level, this preference or 'unconscious bias' bypasses our normal, rational and logical thinking, and is below our awareness.

Fortunately, we now live in a time when we are learning to recognise, understand and master our prejudices or 'pre-judgements'. However, despite our sophistication, we still retain the ability to tap into our instincts; we use our past experiences; we check in with our emotions; we read situations and people; we learn about the contexts in which we find ourselves; we interpret, we construe, we generalise. All these activities are driven by fundamental, primordial questions: *Do I feel safe here? Am I under threat? Can I survive?* If we feel safe, we can trust, and without the need to defend and protect ourselves we are free to be our true selves, connect with others, build relationships and work collaboratively.

So intuitive responses can be used very effectively and can be positive in guiding us away from harmful situations. Even so, we need to remember that these often subconscious responses happen too fast for the brain to process them rationally and logically – and therefore they are not always accurate or helpful. Take the example of interview panels that only appoint people perceived to be 'people like us' (called 'affinity bias'), and thereby miss out on vital opportunities for new perspectives and problem-solving and decision-making skills. Unconscious bias can produce almost unnoticeable behaviours (micro-behaviours) in our interactions with others: paying a little less attention to the other person; addressing them less warmly; talking less frequently to them; lacking empathy with them.

The results of these negative micro-behaviours are small at first, but long-term exposure is corrosive; left unchecked, they take us to the edge of prejudice and poor decision-making and create a culture that is introspective, fearful and blaming.

Unconscious bias revealed: micro-messaging

As we mentioned in Chapter 5, we are constantly interpreting clusters of non-verbal cues alongside the verbal communication; however micro-messages are rather more difficult to decipher. They are elusive, more of a 'gut feeling', like when you're aware of your feelings during a conversation, but you can't really describe what's going on; for example, when you come away feeling undervalued, uncomfortable, undermined, or excluded, but you can't quite explain how or why.

In fact these messages emerge in the gap between the words spoken and the message received, between what was said and what was understood, and although these messages are micro-behaviours, they are very powerful – with potentially long-lasting impact. They convey feelings that inform us whether it's safe to express our views, whether we fit in, feel welcome, feel valued, or feel supported.

The destructive influence of negative micro-inequities

Negative micro-messages (micro-inequities) reinforce prejudice, create 'in-groups' and 'out-groups', leave colleagues feeling undervalued, reduce potential, and inhibit initiative. They promote feelings of unease and exclusion – even a sense of being invisible within the group. Negative micro-messaging is particularly heightened when differences are seen as being dangerous, or when discomfort with the unfamiliar triggers micro-inequities when talking to or about the other person such as dismissive facial expressions, reserved body language, nuanced choices of words and general behaviour indicating lack of interest in that person. In a very short time these subtle, often unconscious, micro-inequities can devalue and discourage individuals and impair team performance.

Micro-messages reveal your core feelings – evident in gestures as small as a nod of the head, an insincere smile, a sideways glance, and the tone and inflection of your voice. Here are some more examples of typical slights and snubs:

> ➤ praising an idea presented by one colleague; ignoring the same idea presented by another

> ➤ checking or sending messages on your phone/ other device while someone is talking to you

> ➤ replying to someone with sarcasm

It can be difficult to be aware of the personal biases we communicate in the form of micro-inequities – getting to know oneself is the work of a lifetime – but being intentional about our communication and being curious about the sources of our emotional responses and 'gut reactions' is a start.

Positive micro-messaging to motivate and inspire

Positive micro-messages (micro-affirmations), on the other hand, can motivate, inspire and enable individuals and teams to stretch their potential and even go beyond expectations. Micro-affirmations are communicated, as you can imagine, through open facial expressions and warm vocal tones, friendly body language, and active, interested listening. They promote feelings of well-being and belonging within the group.

Not only do these micro-affirmations help us to do well and enjoy our work-life, but consistent, appropriate affirmation of others can be contagious – potentially raising morale and productivity of the whole team by modelling affirming behaviour.

Tapping into your bias control mechanism

Although it can be hard to 'catch' yourself unconsciously behaving with bias or sending negative micro-messages, there are some actions you can take – here are a few suggestions for tricking your brain out of its default mode:

> Make a list of your known biases. What sort of person brings them out for you?

> Check whether your language and behaviour really match your values, e.g. if mutual respect and fairness are two of the values that matter to you, how is that made visible in the way you treat those around you?

> Notice whether your greetings, appreciations or congratulations are equally distributed across the team – and monitor your non-verbal communication – is it consistent with everyone?

> Ask yourself whether your humour, including 'jokes' and banter, is really shared by all, or could it come across as hurtful or even aggressive to some colleagues?

> Check that feedback, appraisal conversations, performance reviews, etc. are based on factual and objective observations; during the conversation, monitor your language to ensure that it is clear, moderate and neutral

Tapping into your bias control mechanism in the brain enables you to question automatic responses and prevent biases from becoming behaviour. Effective communicators learn to monitor themselves when in unfamiliar situations, with people they don't know, or with whom they don't seem at first to share much in common. By raising your level of awareness you can become more intentional about choosing micro-affirmations rather than micro-inequities.

Communicating for diversity

If we can't talk openly about our differences, then how will they be honoured and valued? We mentioned earlier that it can sometimes feel difficult to talk about differences between us. It can seem easier to ignore them, or to pretend they don't matter. We can become defensive, falling back on the language of judgement, blame and exclusion... or we can use our conversations as an opportunity for learning and change. In situations where you're feeling a bit uncomfortable, share that observation; if you feel under attack, notice your defensiveness, accept the discomfort and address it. Getting used to doing this is the same as learning to do anything else – it requires a desire to know, motivation to become informed, opportunities to practise and the willingness to correct your mistakes.

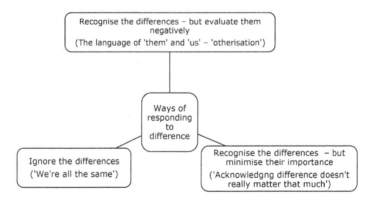

Unhelpful ways of dealing with difference

The habit of forming and maintaining good relationships based on trust and mutual respect stems from the culture of the team, and the organisation. The team's cultural values become embedded as norms of behaviour and – for good or ill – these values are seen, heard and felt in the way that colleagues communicate with each other. We can choose the language that divides or that unites us, that fosters connectedness, interdependence and equality, or separation and inequality. At the same time we need to make room for compassion and forgiveness – of others, yes, but also of ourselves.

No excuses, but we don't always get things right in our relationships with others. Nevertheless, we human beings also have a capacity to be extraordinary – and not just *some* of the time either! When things have gone awry, and you're feeling that somehow you were less than the person you want to be, be kind to yourself and give yourself another chance to get it right.

Here are some steps you could take to build relationships that value diversity in your team:

➢ Publicly acknowledge different values, norms and assumptions

➢ Prepare to accommodate different communication styles

➢ Check out assumptions (yours and theirs)

➢ Attend to 'context' – as always – and perspective (yours and theirs)

➢ Be attentive to verbal and non-verbal cues

➢ Encourage your own enquiring mind and remain open to new learning

➢ Ask questions and listen to the answers

➤ Use humour carefully – does it include or exclude?

➤ Suspend judgement – be aware of personal cultural influences and how they can shape understanding – not always positively or accurately

➤ 'Give permission' to be yourself and extend the same permission to others

Conclusion

We would all like to be seen in the same fine detail in which we think we see ourselves. Respecting diversity means that everyone feels that they are 'seen', valued for who they are, their contribution – at work and in their community. Certain basic needs matter to all of us: the need to feel safe and secure; the need to be respected and feel accepted; the need to be trusted and to be able to trust others; the need to be able to speak openly and to be heard. And of course, diversity is reciprocal; respecting diversity means we act in the best interest of others – and of ourselves.

In this book you've been offered great ideas and suggestions for enhancing your work-life and building good work relationships. Some might argue that this is more straightforward when the team is reasonably homogeneous – after all, it's easier to reach a comfortable consensus when everyone thinks alike – or at least that's how it seems. In reality, making assumptions about shared understanding is at the least lazy and at worst dangerous; dissension is ignored or even punished, important issues are left unexplored, horizons narrowed, possibilities restricted.

Overlooking the richness of diversity is to miss a great opportunity for making the best use of the potential in the team to learn and grow. Respecting diversity makes it possible to benefit from all the voices in the team – and leads to better discussions, and better decision-making. Nevertheless, honouring diversity can be challenging; it means including people with different perspectives, experiences, opinions, and even different working styles or expectations. This also means that good and frequent communication within the team is pivotal, and that takes time.

At times being inclusive in this way will also demand that you be courageous, sometimes changing well-established habits and ways of being – your own or those of others around you. Communication tools will, with practice, help you steer through these challenges. However, to make sure that the tools you have learnt are more than manipulative communication 'tricks', align your communication closely with your values so that everyone in the team feels that they have an equal voice, that they are 'seen' and appreciated, and that they are able to make their full contribution. Remaining true to your best self in this way means you'll be authentic in your connections with others, and build solid relationships based on trust and communication that is clear, respectful and compassionate.

Applying this to your workplace

a) Leveraging diversity for success. Look at the following scenarios:

  ➢ Two new staff members have joined your team; one is Pakistani, one is Sudanese. They spend all their lunch breaks together and seem to be 'outsiders' in the team

  ➢ Two other colleagues find it hard to work together because of how they organise their time; one thinks her colleague is ridiculously rigid about planning and organising their joint projects; the other sees her colleague's 'go with the flow' attitude as chaotic and unproductive

> Another colleague was born and raised in the UK. You notice how he sends negative micro-messages to other team members when a female colleague speaks in meetings

b) In order to make the most of each person's unique personality, what adjustments, changes and conversations would the team have to make? And the individuals concerned? How might you optimize the diversity of your team?

Further references

> Banaji, M. R., *Blindspot: hidden biases of good people*, Bantam, 2016

> Coyne, D., *The culture code: the secrets of highly successful groups*, Random House, 2018

> Guirdham, O. and Guirdham, M., *Communicating across cultures at work*, 4th edition, Red Globe Press, 2017

> Nowak, Martin, *Super co-operators*, Canongate, 2011

> Sarpong, J., *Diversify: a handbook for these troubled times*, HQ, 2019

> Young, Stephen, *Micro-messaging: why great leadership is beyond words*, McGraw-Hill, 2007

The stepping up toolkit: how to succeed as a new manager or leader

Introduction

It can be quite daunting when you are asked to step up to a more senior role. Perhaps you have been asked to manage a project for the first time, or to cover for a colleague who is going on maternity leave, or the 'higher-paid help' have recognised your talents and have asked you to become a team leader or manage a department. One of your first questions is likely to be 'What does this new job involve?'

Before we introduce the starter-kit, take some time to look back at previous chapters of this book. Which chapters will be of most help to you over the short term? Certainly with 'manager' or 'leader' in your job title you need to see your work environment from this new vantage point and with a new mind-set (Chapter 4) as you are now expected, for example, to:

> be more responsible for people

> communicate more frequently with your line manager and on higher-level topics

> be more knowledgeable about your organisation's strategy and policies

> keep close to major clients

➢ communicate well across the organisation

➢ spend time on recruitment and business development

This may prompt you to wonder how you are going to spend more of your working day on the above activities, in which case the tips in Chapter 12 on delegating will be of great help to you. Or perhaps you feel you need to urgently revisit Chapter 8 on influencing or Chapter 15 on diversity.

Whatever it is that you need to revise, we suggest you do this before engaging with this new material.

The stepping up toolkit

This starter-kit for stepping up to a more senior role gives an outline of:

➢ the main scope of a manager's or team leader's role

➢ the stages of team development

➢ ways of assessing your team's performance

➢ some ongoing research on employee engagement

Leadership and management are mainly outside the scope of this book. However, we wanted to share some very useful material with you. You can download this toolkit at www.learningcorporation.co.uk/Library.

Pause for reflection

What are the top 5–10 things you have learned by reading this book?

What are the top 2–5 actions you will take to make your working relationships happier and more effective?

What other key people in your organisation would be interested in reading this book?

Conclusions

Whilst putting the finishing touches to this book, one image that kept popping up in my mind was of a beautiful woven piece of cloth. This cloth was made of many different coloured threads, woven together to form intricate patterns. As the cloth was being woven it was strengthened by cross-threading. Because the cloth was densely woven it is now being made into jackets, strong enough to keep out cold weather.

In a similar fashion, strong working relationships can be built by valuing the uniqueness each team member brings. Each person's talents and strengths can be woven together and strengthened through trust and effective communications. Great relationships can withstand stormy times at work.

This book is very apposite in the world in which we live. First, to restore broken personal relationships. As you have read the book you have probably realised that many of the tips in this book apply equally to our personal lives. Good personal relationships have a beneficial effect on our physical health and our emotional and mental well-being. Building great relationships literally makes us feel better.

Secondly, I'm very conscious that this book will be published at a time when the world is in more turmoil than at any other time in the last 70 years. In these unprecedented times there are signs that nations are withdrawing into their national shells and regressing to a dog eats dog mentality. However, the problems we face nationally and internationally, be they environmental, health, economic, moral, political, or social, can be addressed, but will require innovative solutions. In order to find these, nations will need to apply the same principles that we have been advocating in this book. Here are just two examples:

> to listen patiently and attentively, without judgement, seeking to understand the other nation's point of view

> to recognise that in any situation there are more than two options and by working creatively together and applying new levels of thinking acceptable solutions can be found

You can add other examples from the book.

As Martin Luther King said, *'We must learn to live together as brothers or perish together like fools.'*

Please make full use of the resources in www.learnngcorporation.co.uk/Library and if you are a coach or mentor please also access www.coachingknowhow.com.

Should you require our guidance or support in facilitating workshops or in 1 to 1 coaching please do not hesitate to get in touch.

I would like to end by wishing you an enjoyable and fulfilling working life and relaying a greeting I first received when trekking in Nepal – 'Namaste', which means 'I bow to you, or I acknowledge the divine spark in you'.

Richard Fox
Surrey, England
March 2020

Author's biographical details

Richard Fox, Partner, The Learning Corporation LLP

Richard is an experienced leadership coach, career coach and facilitator and a Master NLP Practitioner. He has an honours degree in law, economics and accountancy. After a career in major consulting practices culminating as a partner in KPMG, he has spent the last 27 years as a partner in a pan-European firm specialising in developing people. He has a deep knowledge of business and management as well as expertise in personal effectiveness, interpersonal skills and team and organisational leadership.

Richard has worked in a wide range of industry sectors, in the public and private sectors and with not-for-profit organisations. He has advised organisations of all sizes from start-ups to global corporations and has worked in over 25 countries.

He is the author of *Creating a purposeful life – how to reclaim your life, live more meaningfully and befriend time* and has contributed chapters in other published books and articles, and he has published two booklets.

Outside work Richard's main interests are designing and leading walks, choral music, socialising, and exploring the natural world. He is a member of St Saviour's Church,

Guildford and has a special interest in meaning and purpose at both the personal and organisational levels.

www.learningcorporation.co.uk
www.purposefullives.com

Anneliese Guérin-LeTendre, Founder Dialogue Links

Anneliese is a leadership coach and intercultural/ interpersonal communications specialist with over 30 years' teaching, training and facilitation experience in the public and private sectors. She has co-authored a guide for doctors coming to work in the UK – *So you qualified abroad* – and is passionate about promoting communication, cultural intelligence and diversity as force multipliers for leaders and their teams.

www.dialoguelinks.co.uk

Printed in the USA
CPSIA information can be obtained
at www.ICGtesting.com
JSHW011539120224
57197JS00020B/468